You Can Be
A Super Quilter!

A Teach-Yourself Manual
For Beginners

Carla J. Hassel

Cover photograph by Bob Calmer

The Pella Tulip Quilt pictured on the cover was appliqued and lap-quilted by fifteen people in five states—Judy Mark, Janis Waldorf, Clara McKinley, Janet Mitchell, Susan Knight, Marilyn Lee, Fran Keller, and Carla Hassel, all of Des Moines, Iowa; Joy Kidney, West Des Moines, Iowa; Dietre McCormick, Carlisle, Iowa; Pam Dyer, Winterset, Iowa; Sue Dietz, Omaha, Nebraska; Judy Gabbert, Dallas, Texas; Sue Ferree, McPherson, Kansas; and Nancy Carter, Greenville, Illinois. Owner: Carla Hassel.

Library of Congress
Catalog Card Number 79-65042
ISBN 0-87069-294-1
Copyright © 1980
Ninth printing, 1986
Carla J. Hassel

Published by

Wallace-Homestead Book Company
580 Water's Edge Road
Lombard, Illinois 60148

To You, the Beginner

I learned to quilt without the help of books or a teacher, as the original quilters did long ago. You could, too, if that were the only way. Your talents and ideas are as good as mine. I want only to help you along by convincing you that you *can* do it, if it is important enough to you, and you *will* do it, if you try. So let us begin at the beginning.

With thanks to my parents, who taught me "where there's a will, there's a way," and to the rest of my team, Gary, Kirsten and David.

Foreword

There are dozens upon dozens of quilting books available today. This one is different. It is not a history of quilting. It is not a collection of photographs of quilts so exquisite, but so impossible, that no beginner would dream of undertaking such a project. It is not a series of diagrams of the 200 best-loved quilt patterns complete with their names, many of which contradict the names given in the next collection of diagrams. Such books overwhelm the beginner and certainly do nothing to support her (or him) in her first efforts at this art form.

Quilting *is* an art form. Therefore, it is my basic assumption that the beginner needs to be taught the simplest *basics* of quilting in such a way as to build her self-confidence and to encourage creativity. History and nomenclature are vital and fascinating aspects of quilting, but the beginner will value these more if she first develops an appreciation for her own talents as an artist.

Whether this manual is used in conjunction with a class or as a home-study device, the reader must consider herself a learner and allow herself to discover the "tools of the trade" in the order in which they are presented. Each recommended project should be undertaken and completed, lest the pupil miss a valuable lesson and suffer the consequences later. As her knowledge increases, the opportunities to be creative and to stray from the manual will become apparent. At no time should she be permitted to suffer defeat—defeat produces quitters.

Above all, I hope this manual encourages the beginner to *think*, to use her *own* judgment, to be innovative, and, above all, to be proud of her accomplishments. My hope is to whet her appetite for quilting, not satiate.

Contents

Foreword 4
How to Use This Manual 6
UNIT I Beginnings
    Chapter 1 Supplies and Demands, or "Getting
      It All Together" 7
    Chapter 2 Nomenclature 13
UNIT II Basic Piecing and Quilting
    Chapter 1 General Piecing and Quilting
      Instructions 15
    Chapter 2 Piecing Squares 27
    Chapter 3 Piecing Triangles, Borders, and
      Cording 35
    Chapter 4 Piecing Hexagons.............. 39
    Chapter 5 Piecing Curves 44
UNIT III Dresden Plate — Pieced and Appliqued . . 47
UNIT IV Lap-Quilting
    Chapter 1 Dresden Plate Quilt 52
COLOR SECTION Completed Projects 65
    Chapter 2 Friendship Quilt 69
UNIT V True Applique 70
UNIT VI Puff-Patch 76
UNIT VII Cathedral and Attic Window 82
UNIT VIII Quilts and Traditional Frame Quilting
    Chapter 1 Designing Your Quilt............. 86
    Chapter 2 The Mathematics of Design 91
    Chapter 3 Determining Fabric Requirements . . 95
    Chapter 4 The Quilt Top 98
    Chapter 5 Frame-Quilting 100
    Chapter 6 Finishing the Quilt 103
Appendix I Jiffy Bias 104
Appendix II Quilting Designs 107
Appendix III Permanent Template Section 110
Appendix IV Helpful Hints 114
Glossary 115
Index 117
About the Author 120
TEAR-OUT TEMPLATE SECTION 121
    Shopping List 121

How to Use This Manual

If you have not already read the foreword, do so now. Then read the chapter on supplies. Take the shopping list from the perforated section in the back of the book and equip your sewing box. Purchase and prepare your fabric for quilting.

Successive lessons are divided into two parts. One section is the written part of this manual. In the back of the book, on perforated pages, you will find the pattern pieces needed for each project. This section is designed to enable you to cut out patterns without defacing the body of the book, at the same time saving you the time it would take to trace them all. Keep a manila envelope inside the back cover; glue it in, if you like. Label and place the used templates in the envelope for future use. If the templates *do* become lost, you may trace new patterns from the permanent template section at the very back of the book, just as you would trace templates from any other book.

But by all means, *do* cut out the original templates from the perforated section—this book was specifically designed to eliminate time and trouble.

Each lesson is independent of the others. The cost-conscious quilter may choose to buy several yards of fabric and make all the projects from one batch of material. Others may have a specific plan for each project and make a separate shopping trip for each lesson.

Some beginners never plan to make an entire quilt. Often someone needs a few gift ideas and likes to work with her hands, but needs some elementary guidelines for some simple projects. The pillows and placemats in the beginning lessons are perfect.

Other beginners are eager to begin that first quilt the minute they start, and pillows seem to be a waste of time. After she has pieced and appliqued a few beginning projects, the quilt enthusiast will be better able to select fabrics and apply basic techniques as she undertakes the expensive and laborious task of quilt-making, and with much more satisfying results.

Still other beginners have no desire to piece or applique. They simply desire to learn "quick and easy, perfect, 10-stitch-to-the-inch quilting in one simple lesson," so that an unfinished family heirloom can be quilted. I shudder to think that after years in the attic a fine (or maybe not so fine) quilt top might be the object of someone's very first attempt at quilting. It is nice to be able to look back on our first efforts and smile at our lack of expertise, but there is also a certain joy in replacing that first attempt with better work. I would not want my first irregular and oversized quilting stitches there on great-grandmother's quilt, haunting me forever! So even if you intend to end your quilting career after one heirloom, please spend a few weeks learning to make a pillow top or two. After you realize the time and love grandma put into *her* quilt top, you will find much more satisfaction and joy as you add your own time and love in the quilting process.

Step-by-step, let us begin with expectation and enthusiasm.

UNIT I Beginnings
Chapter 1 / Supplies and Demands, or "Getting It All Together"

Supplies for the Sewing Box. The first thing you need to do is find a box, a sturdy one with a tight-fitting lid. An antique cigar box lends a nice touch to your quilting image, and everyone will naturally assume you are an avid quilter with years of experience. Otherwise, a fruitcake tin, lock-top food storage container, or medium-sized shoebox (complete with a rubber band for securing purposes) would do nicely. A sturdy box which will not dump its contents in the snow when it is dropped is the first secret to portable quilting.

The second secret is this: Keep all the supplies for the box *in* the box, even if it means buying duplicates of things usually kept in the kitchen or sewing room. Good scissors aren't cheap, but neither is your time. Don't spend it running back and forth and all over the house looking for your supplies. End of lecture.

To make life unbelievably simple, a shopping list has been included in the perforated "cutout" section. Included here are explanations to accompany that list.

Sewing Box. Find a sturdy, but lightweight, box of carrying size with a tight-fitting lid. If square or rectangular, it should be about 8″ x 8″ or 8″ x 10″. It must be at least 2½″ deep to accommodate spools of thread and a pin-cushion. If it is circular, it must be at least 8″ in diameter to accommodate a 6″ ruler and scissors.

Needles. When you shop for needles, you will find that there are many varieties and sizes available. You are probably most familiar with *sharps*. For quilting, you will purchase *betweens* (sometimes marked "quilting"). A "between" needle is the same thickness as a sharp needle of a given size, but it is about ¼″ shorter. The shorter, stubby needle is easier to handle as you work through the layers at the quilting stage, and it is less likely to bend or break. As the size of the needle increases, whether it is a sharp or a between, the length of the needle decreases and the thickness decreases. Therefore, if you were to place a 7 sharp beside a 10 between, you would notice a considerable difference.

A beginner should purchase one package of sharps, either size 7 or 8, but she would be wise to purchase several packages of betweens: 7, 8, and 9, if they are available. In the piecing stages, you may use whatever needle feels comfortable, because the strength of your piecing lies in the *type* of stitching, not solely in the *tininess* of your stitches. Use the 7 between needle for your first attempts at quilting, because the length of the needle will not be so drastically unfamiliar to your hands. As your quilting stitch improves in character, and you become a fanatic on the size of your stitches, switch to the 8 between. You *may* notice a difference. If you are so lucky as to find 9 and 10 betweens, you may experiment with them, too.

Pins. Quilters take note of this frightful misconception: The bigger and fatter the pin the better it will hold fabric. Not true! In fact, the bigger and fatter the pin, the more awkward it will be to handle, the less precise the pinning will be, and the bigger the holes in the fabric will be. The only good thing I can say about 2″ pins is that one is easily found on the carpet after it falls to the floor.

Fine pins make smaller holes, slide into the fabric more easily, and define a stitching line more accurately. The pins with the colored plastic heads have one more marvelous advantage: the thread doesn't catch on the heads as you sew.

Your pins should be about 1″ long and no thicker than a size 8 between needle. Size 17 ballpoint pins are perfect, with dressmaker pins, sizes 17 or 20, a good second choice.

Scissors. Many five-year-olds are already aware that some scissors are for paper and others are for sewing. Did your mother ever scold you for using the dressmaker shears for cutting the coupon from a cereal box? Needless to say, the cardboard-template cutting a quilter does makes it imperative that she keep two pairs of scissors handy.

A small pair of scissors (the fold-up variety, perhaps) is a nice addition to the sewing box, for thread cutting. The larger scissors need not be ever-present at the quilter's side, since most template-making and fabric-cutting is done at home, and good scissors are too expensive to have duplicates.

For the sewing box, purchase one small pair of scissors with sharp tips. For use at home, purchase good dressmaking scissors and not-so-good "paper" scissors.

Thread. For piecing and applique, common sewing thread is used. Whatever you have will do nicely. For your sewing box, a few colors will do—yellow, blue, red, and green. The piecing thread need not match the fabric exactly. For applique, depending on the fineness of your stitching and the type of stitching you are using, you will do better to match the thread to the fabric color. To keep the thread from tangling, run each piece of the thread over a piece of beeswax.

Quilting thread is becoming a readily available commodity, even in colors. A beginner should purchase white for quilting her first projects. Stitches in colored quilting thread attract too much attention: therefore, colored quilting thread should not be used by anyone whose stitches are not reasonably regular. Even white stitches on navy blue do not appear as obvious as colored stitches on white. Do not take this warning *too* seriously. It is not necessary to purchase colored quilting thread to avoid quilting on chocolate brown or navy blue with your white quilting thread. Simply ignore the fact that you are a beginner and confidently use the white thread as though you have been quilting for years.

If your thread tangles and knots terribly, and if colored quilting thread is available, you may choose to use quilting thread for piecing and applique as well as quilting. Keep in mind that the thread is thicker and that corners, with their high concentration of stitches, may tend to be bulky.

Beeswax. Running your 18″ pieces of thread over a piece of beeswax before you thread the needle will help diminish tangling.

Fabric Markers. The most important marking you will be doing as a beginner is the marking of the pieces to be cut for piecing. Because these markings are on the *wrong side of the fabric*, a hard pencil (#2½ or #3) may be used. Pencil does not wash out, so keep in mind that it should be used only on the wrong side of the fabric.

Dark fabrics present a problem. A yellow or white colored pencil sometimes leaves a clear marking. Often, a quilter will use a ball-point pen to mark dark fabrics on the wrong side. It is essential to test the ink's properties regarding washing. If the ink "bleeds," it will ruin light fabrics in the quilt top. If it seems permanent, it may be used freely on the *dark* fabrics only. If the ink shows through to the right side of a light-colored fabric, it will be a permanent eyesore on the right side of the finished top. If a mistake in judgment has been made, and ink either bleeds or a line shows on the right side, spray the area with hair spray and wash it under running water — you may be lucky enough to have the ink wash out.

The wonderful, new, cold-water, washable felt-tip pen is marvelous. It is recently available in most areas. Its ink flows easily onto the fabric, and distortion in the marking process is therefore reduced. It is safe for marking both the wrong and right sides of fabrics, so it is ideal for marking applique designs and elaborate quilting designs. Cold water will make the ink disappear, but it is always wise to test any marker on each fabric *to be safe.* The only drawback I know, as far as this pen is concerned, is that after a few very humid summer days, the markings on a quilt had disappeared. This problem could be eliminated by storing quilt pieces or completed blocks in plastic bags when they are temporarily out of use.

In the "olden days," powdered bluing was used to mark quilting designs. The desired quilt design was cut away from a piece of cardboard, window-template style (see Index). On elaborate designs the quilting line appeared broken in places, because bridges of cardboard had to be left to connect the sections of the cardboard to one another. When the template was placed on the quilt top the fabric showed only where the quilting was to be. The powder was dusted onto the template. When the template was removed, the quilting lines were clearly marked. A finer template was made by punching a line of holes in paper using a pin. The unthreaded needle of the sewing machine did this job quickly. This information is interesting, in a historical sense, but the process is too time-consuming for the modern quilter who has a washable pen at her disposal.

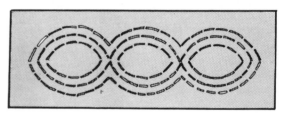

Window template for quilt design

Design left in powdered bluing

Most beginning quilting will not require extensive marking. However, the marking of uniform designs on the entire quilt is within the near future of some beginners. For them a combination of old and new techniques is suggested: a lightweight cardboard template should be cut (window-style); the marking could quickly and easily be done with the washable pen.

Rulers. Two sizes will be needed — 6″ and 18″. Either a simple plastic 6″ ruler with 1/16″ markings or a more sophisticated version with a sliding marker is a vital part of the sewing box. The metal 6″ ruler with the sliding marker is usually called a hem or knitting gauge. Most of your projects will require measurements greater than 12″. A yardstick is too cumbersome for routine use; therefore, purchase an 18″ ruler to be kept handy.

Tape Measure. The cloth tape measures are not really reliable, but the extra length is convenient for ruffle cutting and quilt measuring when extreme accuracy is not vital.

Pincushion. Choose one of appropriate size for your sewing box.

Thimble. Even if you have never used a thimble, purchase one which will fit the middle finger of your sewing hand. The thimble is used to push the needle through the fabric as you sew, not to keep the finger on the other hand from being poked. An inexpensive metal thimble is your best buy, but more expensive leather thimbles are preferred by many quilters.

If you simply *must* have the best, buy a leather thimble with a small metal insert for extra protection. Leather will stretch, so the thimble should be plenty snug when you try it on at the store. If the thimble becomes much too loose, a small tuck can be made on the fingernail side of the thimble, preferably by a shoe repairman's sewing machine and not yours!

Seam Ripper. Purchase an extra one for your sewing box.

Clasp-closing Manila Envelope. A 6½″ x 9½″ envelope is ideal for template storage. Glue it inside the cover of this book for a truly organized approach.

Extra Supplies. In the excitement of gathering up your supplies, you may want to add a few extra things which will aid your creativity.

Colored Pencils. Colored pencils or felt-tip markers will help you experiment with color and design.

Graph Paper. Although no enlarging is required for the beginning sections of this book, you may enjoy experimenting with design or may decide you would like to begin enlarging your own templates. Graph paper with ¼″ divisions with extra-dark lines at the 1″ divisions is ideal.

Loose-Leaf Binder. A loose-leaf notebook is ideal to hold your ever-increasing collection of magazine articles and pictures, patterns, and photographs.

Lined Notebook. Purchase a steno pad in which to record the date and place of purchase of your new quilting fabrics. Complete with small swatches of each fabric. This record will be invaluable should you ever run short of a fabric.

Fabrics for Tops

Types of Fabrics. It was not too long ago that polyesters virtually eliminated quilters' cottons from the fabric store. Double-knits and bonded fabrics were in vogue, and the quilter who wanted strictly 100 percent cotton broadcloths met with great frustration. At that time it was decided that cottons and cotton/polyester blend fabrics could be used together in a quilt top *if* all of them had been preshrunk. A decade has passed, and 100 percent cotton is again readily available in many beautiful colors and prints.

To make a basic rule, let us say that broadcloth-weight cottons and blends may be used together. The blends sometimes seem very sheer, especially solid whites and creams, and oftentimes have a directional sheen. This sheen can create a hodgepodge appearance if the pieces are not cut all in one direction (as with napped fabrics in dressmaking). Experience will be the best teacher. Furthermore, cottons do not ravel as much as blends, and blends ravel more as the percentage of polyester in the fabric increases.

Do not buy corduroys, wools, knits, real dotted swiss (with raised dots), satiny fabrics, sheer fabrics, felts, denims, or fabrics with a printed patchwork pattern. These fabrics may be lovely for machine-made wall hangings, bibs, and clothing ornamentation, but for handwork they create too many problems and are not suitable for traditional quilting.

Avoid fabrics which have a noticeable amount of finishing. The fabric feels stiff and may continue to be stiff after washing. It is difficult to stitch and virtually impossible to "straighten."

Prints and Solids. Prints can be combined very effectively with solids or with other prints. There are just a few basic guidelines to be offered, mainly because choice of fabric is more an aspect of art than of technique. In order not to stifle creativity, but to

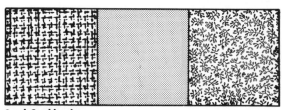

Good Combination

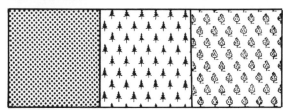

Poor Combination

eliminate some beginning frustration, a few statements should be made:

1 Choose prints that vary in scale.

2 Vary the theme of the print—too many rose-buds are too many rosebuds. An occasional maple leaf or feather would be nice.

3 Experiment with prints that have different color harmonies. Make something splashy once in a while.

4 Tiny dotted swiss fabric (printed dots, not raised dots) has the effect of a solid color. From a distance the dots disappear, but a "texture" is given to the fabric that is richer than a plain solid of the same color. However, never use two dotted swiss fabrics together in a two-fabric project—your eyes will have a difficult time focusing.

5 Assign a printed fabric its color characteristic based on the color of the background, or by the total impact of the colors of the figures. Observing a fabric from a distance of two yards through squinted eyes will help you determine the overall color of a print.

6 Avoid gingham as a beginner. The fact that half of the color of the fabric is white makes the colored part "wash out." This is especially true of pastel ginghams. An extra drawback is that it really should be considered a "directional fabric," requiring special attention in the fabric-marking process.

The scale of a print must correspond to the size of the cut piece of fabric. As a guideline, avoid a fabric if at least one repeat of the print will not be contained in a pattern piece.

Suffice it to say, all of these statements have their drawbacks. Therefore, they are "guidelines" and not "rules." For example, in a Grandmother's Flower Garden quilt, all flowered prints would be delightful. The point is, be flexible, try new things, and prove the rest of us wrong.

Preparing the Fabrics
For Piecing and Quilting

The fabrics must be prepared in two ways before they are marked and cut. First the fabric must be tested for colorfastness, lest a fabric bleed its color onto a finished quilt project. The second step in preparation is to preshrink the fabric before fabrics of different fiber contents are sewn together. Fabric of 100 percent cotton fibers shrinks more than a blend of 35 percent cotton/65 percent polyester; therefore, puckering of the seams will be the result if fabric is used without preshrinking.

Selvages shrink more because of their higher thread count and should be eliminated in the marking and cutting process. Never trust a label which boasts "colorfast—preshrunk." Better to be safe than to be sorry.

Colorfastness. To test for colorfastness, soak each fabric individually in a basin of very warm water for 15 minutes. Swish the fabric around and then wring it out. If the water remains clear, the fabric is colorfast and may be tossed into the washing machine for preshrinking. If the water is discolored, the fabric fails the test and needs further treatment.

The easiest treatment for a non-colorfast fabric is simply to eliminate it from your quilt. If that fails to be a likable solution, the fabric must be treated to make the colors fast. You may "cook" the fabric for 15 minutes in vinegar water (Easter-egg style) or soak the fabric in very warm salt water (one tablespoon per gallon) for an hour. After either salt or vinegar treatment, the questionable fabric should be washed with something white to assure success. If your favorite fabric is still giving you problems, wash it over and over again with a new "something white" each time. Five or six washings may bring satisfactory results, otherwise set the fabric aside and live with your disappointment.

Preshrinking. Divide your fabrics into lights and darks for preshrinking. Wash the fabric as you would the finished product: warm water, soap, fabric softener, and regular agitation. Dry the fabrics in the dryer if you plan to dry the finished product in the dryer. If the fabrics are 1/8 yard or smaller scraps, wash in a net laundry bag to decrease tangling.

Unless you need the fabrics before laundry day, it usually works well to throw a few pieces in the machine with each load of wash (after they have been tested for colorfastness!). If more than four or five ¼-yard and ½-yard pieces are thrown in together, an incredible tangle is sure to result.

One helpful hint suggests that the fabrics be put through the rinse cycle only, since the fabrics are not soiled. I feel it is safer to use the full cycle, testing the fabric under routine washing conditions.

Bias and Straightening the Fabric. Dressmakers are well aware of the problems seamstresses can have with bias. Lengthwise grain, cross grain and bias are the three terms which describe the direction of the thread in the fabric. Cross grain refers to the threads running from selvage to selvage. Lengthwise grain refers to the threads running parallel to the selvages and perpendicular to the cross grain. If you pull on either of these grains, the fabric will not "give." If, however, you pull diagonally on the fabric, there will be considerable stretch. This diagonal is the bias, and you will notice

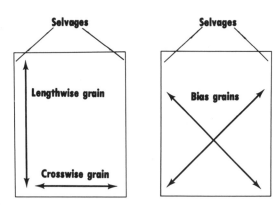

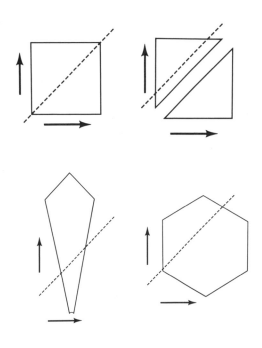

Common quilting pieces, showing cross grain, lengthwise grain and bias (dotted lines)

that the bias can run in two directions. At times this stretch is desirable; at other times this stretch creates problems.

In order to control this stretch, the seamstress must ascertain whether the fabric is straight. That is to say, whether the cross grain and the lengthwise grain are truly perpendicular to each other. If the fabric is not straight, the situation can be corrected. Obviously, the technique is called "straightening," and is done by pulling on the bias line that will bring the cross grain and lengthwise grain threads into proper alignment. (See figures.)

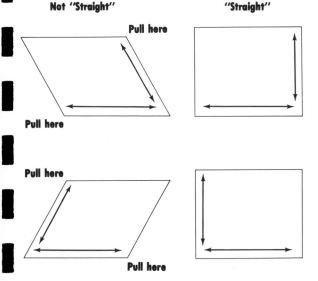

If you are accustomed to straightening fabric, by all means continue to do so with your quilting fabrics. If you are not, however, and fail to understand how this is done, be assured that you can still be a quilter. Because quilters use such small units of fabric in the first place, and oftentimes scraps too small to straighten, this straightening isn't terribly important. If a definite print

runs slightly off-grain, the pieces should be cut in alignment with the print. As you gain piecing experience, you will discover that it is nice to have squares that lie on the grain line, and triangles, too, can easily be cut "square" on the fabric. But a hexagon will automatically have true bias edges, and Dresden Plate has edges which are not true anything. In other words, if worrying about it helps, worry about it; if it doesn't, don't.

Ironing the Fabric. Some fabrics come out of the dryer ready to cut. Others will need ironing. If a fabric is really wrinkled, you may decide to reject it from your quilting fabrics. Any fabric which does not wash nicely as yard goods will not wash nicely as a quilt piece.

Quilt Batting. The batting is the layer between the top and the bottom of the quilt. The batting adds the warmth and weight and makes the quilting stitches more than simple stitches on a flat surface.

11

If you were to examine several old quilts, you would find more than one type of batting. Cotton was surely the most common, complete with seeds. It is not unusual to find an old woolen blanket put to good use between quilt top and quilt backing. Other "quilts" were made by layering fabrics to create a heavy quilt top and had no batting or quilting stitches at all.

Contemporary quilters usually choose polyester batting. It is available in a fluffy layer ¼" to 2" thick, or a thin, tightly-woven "thermal blanket" style. Some is just plain thin! A good product for a beginner is the fluffier type, ¼" to ½" thick. Polyester is preferable to cotton because it is very cohesive. It washes nicely and does not shift in the finished product. Manufacturers recommend "wash-warm, line-dry." Most quilters find the performance is satisfactory if they machine wash on the gentle cycle and dry in the dryer using a low heat setting.

If you prefer cotton batting, you will find it is generally less expensive than polyester, but you must be prepared to put more quilting in the finished product to avoid shifting.

A twin bed size, 81" x 96" will be sufficient for the small projects. More can be purchased for the lap-quilt at a later date.

Quilt Backing. The most important feature of quilt backing is its "quiltability." Will the quilting needle glide in and out easily, or will each stitch take effort? How pretty the backing is must be a secondary factor.

Extra-wide fabric is sold for quilting under the name "sheeting" or "quilt backing." It is loosely woven; that is, it has a low thread count, with adequate spacing between the threads for the quilting needle. Use of a real *sheet* made of percale, with its very high thread count (up to 180 threads per square inch), would result in great difficulties for a quilter. Quilt backing, or muslin sheeting, 80" to 90" wide is ideal for full-sized quilt projects, and its definite lack of personality actually enhances the beauty of the quilt design on the backside of the quilt.

In pillows, the quilt backing itself is not visible, so beauty is of no consideration and any loosely woven fabric will do nicely. On pot holders, placemats, and baby bibs, the quilter may choose to use fabric matching the quilt top to create a reversible product. Because the project is small, and will be quilted without a frame, a more tightly woven fabric will not present too great a problem compared to the added beauty it will give to the finished product.

Whatever quilt backing you choose, preshrink and color test it as you would fabric for the quilt top, ironing it if necessary.

A yard of 80" to 90" wide muslin sheeting should be sufficient for the small projects. If it is not available locally, it can be ordered from large department store catalogs.

Polyester Filling. Bags of polyester filling will be needed for pillow stuffing. Because it is washable-dryable, it can be sewn permanently into pillows. It does not mildew and fluffs nicely with each washing.

Foam rubber stuffing is not recommended. Because it is difficult to achieve *exact* measurements in quilted pillowtops, preformed pillow inserts are not practical.

Template Cardboard. Recipe cards or index cards are the perfect weight for templates used for small quilting projects. You would be wise to buy one sheet of poster board, 32" x 40" wide, for use in the lap-quilting section.

Chapter 2 / Nomenclature

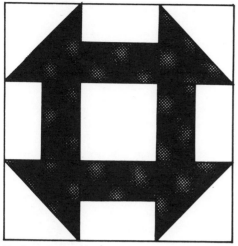

Monkey Wrench

Monkey Wrench is a simple pattern, and one that is beautifully done in the scrapbag style. It is a very common pattern, one that should be known by all, it seems. But the simple Monkey Wrench, without being changed at all, is also the Double Monkey Wrench. To some, it is Love Knot, Hole-in-the-Barn-Door, Lincoln's Platform, or Sherman's March. Two more names are Puss-in-the-Corner and Shoo-Fly.

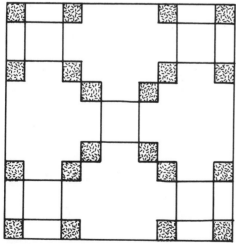

Puss-in-the-Corner

Puss-in-the-Corner is a very descriptive name, so much so that several quilts go by the name. Shoo-Fly has the same honor, creating confusion in a conversation unless all of the quilters participating are aware of the problem.

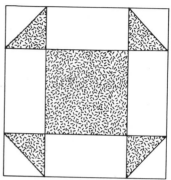

Puss-in-the-Corner
Kitty-Corner, Tic-Tac-Toe

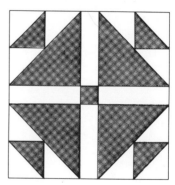

Shoo-Fly
Duck and Ducklings, Corn and Beans, Handy Andy, Hen and Chickens

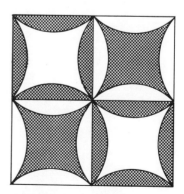

Robbing Peter to Pay Paul I
Dolly Madison's Workbox

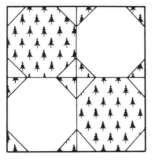

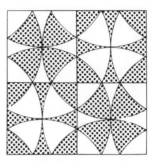

Robbing Peter to Pay Paul II
Octagon

Robbing Peter to Pay Paul III
Winding Ways

Robbing Peter to Pay Paul is a good example of a name which refers to a basic style as well as to a definite pattern. Both Peter-Paul I and Peter-Paul II are made from blocks in which the two fabrics are reversed to make a positive-negative design. Peter-Paul III uses the technique of reversing fabrics and is also known as Winding Ways. Peter-Paul I, by far the most commonly accepted version, is also called Dolly Madison's Workbox. To throw another "monkey wrench" into the mess, you will have the opportunity to piece and quilt Robbing Peter to Pay Paul IV in the lesson on piecing triangles.

Another interesting point is that a single unit of a pattern may have one name, while the various ways of combining the units have specific names. Drunkard's Path is the name of the basic 2-piece unit as well as one arrangement of the units. Using fabrics in equal combinations, several arrangements have specific names. Other designs, such as Steeplechase and Love Ring, take more planning and combine several colors or an uneven usage of fabrics to yield very intricate patterns.

In the midst of all of this, how does the novice begin to approach nomenclature? I suggest she adopt a permissive attitude and enjoy the confusion. The intolerant quilter becomes a bore ("Well, *mine* is Robbing Peter to Pay Paul, and I don't know where you got the silly notion that *yours* is!), and her airs of superiority spoil the fun for the rest of us.

Quilting and individuality should go hand in hand, so take everything with a grain of salt and enjoy yourself!

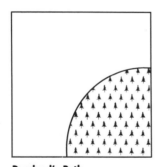

Drunkard's Path
Basic Unit

Love Ring
Nonesuch

Drunkard's Path
Robbing Peter to Pay Paul V,
Rocky Road to Dublin, Rocky Road
to California, Country Husband

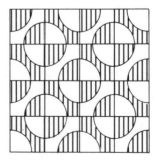

Steeplechase
Bows and Arrows

14

UNIT II Basic Piecing and Quilting
Chapter 1 / General Piecing and Quilting Instructions

Squares are really the most fundamental of all piece-work. You will learn very quickly how to mark your fabric, how to cut quickly and efficiently, and how to piece accurately. Immediately you will become aware of the many opportunities to experiment with design and color.

The mini-pillow (or hot pad) is a quick project that requires so little fabric that you may be able to piece it from scraps. If you choose to make the full-sized pillow, you will need to spend a few extra minutes in planning time before you select the fabrics. Don't allow yourself to become too fussy about "just the right color-match" at this point. The important thing in the beginning is to develop and perfect the basic techniques; color sense and dramatic effect are challenges for the more experienced quilter.

General Instructions — Squares

Preparing the Fabric. Preshrink the fabrics for piecing, the quilt backing, the pillow backing, and lace or ready-made bias tape. Remember that while some people customarily preshrink using the rinse cycle only, it is wisest to wash all of the component parts (with the exception of batting and stuffing, of course) just as you plan to wash the finished project. Dry the materials as you will dry the finished project.

Eliminate any fabrics that seem unsuitable for quilting, particularly those which have raveled or wrinkled considerably. Iron the fabrics lightly and trim all of the selvages.

Cutting the Templates. Cut the paper template from the perforated section of the book. *It is actual size.* It is important to cut exactly on the lines and to keep the corners square. For a project requiring so few as a dozen pieces from any one template, this paper template will suffice.

For projects requiring more than a dozen pieces, there are several approaches to template-cutting. The quilter may cut one, two, or a dozen extra paper templates or make more durable templates which will withstand large-scale usage. The simplest method is to cut several templates from lightweight cardboard. Recipe or index cards are ideal for small templates; cereal box cardboard is a handy choice for large ones.

To make a cardboard template, lay the paper template you have cut from the template section of the book on the cardboard and draw around it. Simple! But as simple as it is, this can be the cause of many, many headaches at the piecing stage. You must hold the marking pen exactly perpendicular (straight up and down) to the edge of the paper template as you draw; if the marking utensil is not a fine point, you may need to slant it slightly inward so that the tip lies snugly against the paper edge. If you do not use caution, the cardboard template will be larger than the original paper template. If it is likely that several cardboard templates will be needed, it is best to cut them all from the original paper template rather than from a new or worn cardboard. Marking a secondary cardboard template from a fresh cardboard template will make the second template larger still, and using a worn template (paper or cardboard) will result in inaccuracy.

You may check the accuracy of your cardboard template by drawing around it on a sheet of paper. Lay the original paper template upon the marked design. The lines should show, but there should be no visible gap between the edge of the paper template and the marked line. If there is, correct your cardboard template.

The most durable template is one cut from lightweight plastic, such as a coffee can lid. Such a template will endure innumerable markings. However, there is a tendency for these templates to be much larger than they should be, and the process of marking the fabric tends to enlarge the pieces completely out of proportion. The solution is to employ extreme caution every step of the way: Draw carefully, cut carefully, and always verify the size of the template.

Many quilters cut templates from sandpaper. If the template is placed sandy-side down on the fabric, slipping on the fabric is kept to a minimum. Feel free to experiment as you wish.

Obviously, one should not mark part of the fabric with one type of template and the rest with another. Don't be reluctant to replace a used template with a fresh one. The most efficient system for pillow-sized projects is simply this:

1 Cut out the paper template.
2 Make one or two cardboard templates from it.
3 Store the original paper template for future reference.
4 Discard the used cardboard templates as they become worn.

The quickest marking system for large-scale projects is achieved by the use of a *multi-template*. The time spent making the multi-template is not justifiable unless there will be more than a hundred pieces cut from one template. The procedure will be discussed along with window templates in the chapter on hexagons.

The type of marking utensil used to mark the fabric will greatly influence the lifespan of your templates, as well as how "heavy the hand" doing the marking. A paper template will endure 6 to 20 markings under normal circumstances, a cardboard one about 40, and a plastic one an indefinite number. Always label your templates and save them for future reference.

IMPORTANT NOTE: *All of the templates you will be using are actual size.* The allowances for seams are not contained in the template itself, but they will "appear" during the marking and cutting procedure.

Marking the Fabric for Cutting. Choose your marking utensil according to your fabric (see page 8) and test the marker on the specific fabric you are planning to use.

YOU ARE GOING TO MARK ONLY THE STITCHING LINE! Some instructors direct the students to mark only the cutting line (!) and not the stitching line — alas, so few of us can stitch perfectly ¼" from the edge, turning corners and following curves. Other instructors would have you make two templates, one actual size (stitching line) and one larger to allow for seams (cutting line). Oh, the drudgery of drawing all the larger pieces, only to go back and insert the smaller template in the center of each so that the stitching line can be added. The beginner who takes all of this quite seriously and painstakingly determines the exact center of each piece before tracing around the smaller template would surely be driven to frustration in no time.

THE ONLY IMPORTANT LINE IS THE STITCHING LINE! That is the one you are going to mark. The secret to happy quilting is this: Minimize the tedium if doing so does not affect quality. Maximum precision, minimum boredom — hooray! Mark your fabric quickly but accurately in the following manner:

1 Mark on the wrong side of the fabric.
2 Place the cardboard template ¼" from the left and top edges of the fabric. (Of course, the selvages have been trimmed away. Right?)
3 Using the least pressure necessary, draw along the edge of the template. Be gentle at the corners to save wear and tear on the template, but be certain that the marking *does* go completely to the edge.
4 Check to be certain that the corners are clearly marked. As you gain experience, you will find that *the line between the corners is actually less important than the corners themselves.*
5 Pick up the template and lay it on the fabric ½" away to the right of the first marked piece. Draw around it. This ½" space will become two ¼" seam allowances upon cutting. If you are not terrific at judging distances, it would be better to leave *more than* ½" than less. You will have the opportunity to trim any excess seam allowance at the piecing stage. Continue marking the first row of pieces.
6 Start a second row of pieces ½" below the first row. NOTE: Always, always stop to think before marking the first piece — using the fabric to your best advantage will assure having sufficient material and reduce expensive waste (and frustration).

The dotted lines in the diagrams are imaginary and indicate the cutting lines.

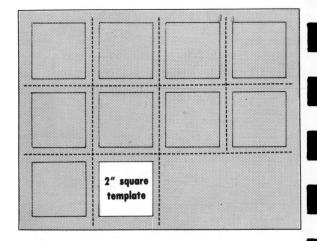

2" square template

Proper spacing for fabric marking (wrong side of fabric)

Squares are lovely for the beginner because the lines follow the natural weave of the fabric, so that there is no need to be concerned about bias in these early stages. Anytime a stripe or definite one-way design is being used, extreme caution must be exercised and sometimes elaborate planning must be done before marking is begun. Save such challenging fabrics for later!

Cutting the Pieces. DO NOT CUT ON THE LINES! First cut between the rows of pieces to make a long strip of pieces. Then cut the individual pieces apart. Notice that each slash of the scissors cuts *two* edges, saving even more time.

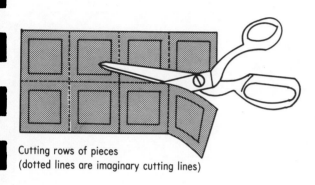

Cutting rows of pieces
(dotted lines are imaginary cutting lines)

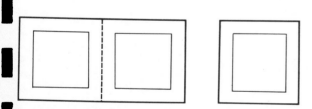

Cutting pieces from rows

It is best to mark and cut out all the pieces for your project before you begin to piece. Lay the pieces in the desired arrangement. Now is the time to change your mind if the colors or designs are not combining to your satisfaction. If you like what you have, you are ready to piece.

Stacking and Threading. Should you be cutting out more than one project at a time, or if you are cutting out the pieces for a quilt, you will save yourself time and trouble at a later moment if you will "stack and thread" the pieces together:

1 Stack all the pieces needed for each project or block in individual piles.
2 Thread a needle and knot only one end.
3 Run this knotted single thread up, back down, and up again through the pile to secure them together.
4 Cut the thread without knotting it, leaving about 2″ of extra thread.

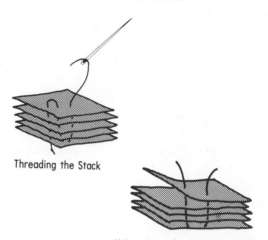

Threading the Stack

Using pieces from the threaded stack

When you are ready to piece, simply snip off the knot at the bottom of the stack and pull that end up to the top of the stack. You will be able to pull off one piece at a time as you would paper from a spindle. Please notice that if you are really clever and arrange the pieces in the sequence in which they will be pieced, with the last piece on the bottom, and if you always start threading the stack from the bottom, you will be able to piece in order without referring to a diagram. No lost pieces!

Experience will teach you to use this technique very effectively, and sometimes you may choose to subdivide the pieces for one project into many stacks. We will talk more about this in specific instances in following lessons.

Piecing

Pinning Two Pieces Together. There are two common approaches to precision piecing. One, usually called the English form, requires a paper template for each fabric piece. A paper template is placed in the center of the cut fabric piece. Then the seam allowances are folded over and basting stitches are taken through all the thicknesses. To join two pieces together, one places two basted paper/fabric pieces side-by-side and carefully blindstitches them together. The time-consuming blindstick must be used so that the pieces will lie flat after stitching. After all the pieces have been joined, the basting threads are removed and the paper templates are discarded. Marking and cutting time are doubled because a paper template is needed for *every* fabric piece. Extra time is also needed for basting and "un-basting." This is a common method for the piecing of hexagons and diamonds, which have bias edges.

The second most common instructions for accurate piecing are these: Sew the pieces together accurately, making sure the edges match. Be extra careful when you sew curves. Here lies the beginner's dilemma. She

has been warned to be "extra careful" and has had fear and trembling stricken into her fingers, but she has been left without any solution to her problem.

This most fundamental aspect of all piecework cannot be dealt with so quickly. If one corner does not match, the next one will not match. If one piece is improperly joined, the row will not properly join with the next row. Here we have the beginnings of a waste of time and a befuddled and discouraged quilter.

In order to eliminate the paper cutting and basting of the first method and to clarify the second method, the two-pin method was devised. It only takes a minute to learn and repays you with many saved minutes throughout your quilting career.

Two-Pin Method

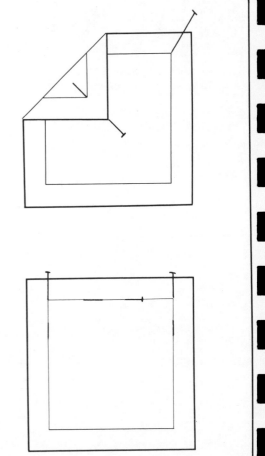

1 Place the pieces being joined right sides together.
2 Insert a pin into the top fabric exactly at the right-hand corner of the stitching line.
3 Flip the two pieces over so that you are able to see the bottom fabric. Push the point of the pin through the bottom fabric exactly at *its* right-hand corner stitching line.
4 Do not bring the pin back through the top fabric. Instead, let the first pin serve as a pivot point while you line up the two stitching lines along the tops of the two squares.
5 Insert the second pin in the left-hand corner of the stitching line of the top fabric. Turn back the left-hand corners of the pieces and slide the bottom piece into place.
6 Push the pin through the bottom fabric at the corner of the stitching line and secure it. Notice that the pin lies exactly on the left-hand, up-and-down seamline and goes through both pieces exactly on the line.
7 Now secure the first pin, using the same technique to align the up and down seamline on the right-hand side.

Two pins should be sufficient for a straight 2″ seam. For a longer seam, add extra pins horizontally in the middle after you have secured both ends.

This pinning method insures exact corners; exact corners virtually insure uniform blocks and a "square" quilt. After you have gained sufficient expertise, you will learn the shortcut "one-pin method."

Choosing the Order in Which
Pieces Are Joined

Squares are ideal for the beginner's first project because only one mistake is possible in the piecing process. The safety rule is this: Always join pieces to form straight lines. Never create a right angle (L-shaped) piecing situation.

Suppose you are making a simple nine-patch. Starting in the upper left-hand corner, join pieces to form vertical rows. Then join the vertical rows to form the finished unit. THE BEGINNER MUST AVOID CREATING A RIGHT ANGLE.

Log Cabin is an old and popular pattern combining squares and rectangles. In this case, one does not piece rows, but begins in the center and pieces outward. Notice that even in this instance, the right-angle theory still applies. The diagrams indicate that pieces are joined to maintain a square or rectangular shape as the design builds.

The simple rule is this: Whether you are working in rows or building from the center, add each piece to maintain the square or rectangular shape. *Do not create an L-shaped corner.*

Note: Of course it is possible to create horizontal rows instead of vertical rows or to start on the right side instead of the left, but we need to keep things uniformly simple. Furthermore, it is not *always* possible to avoid the right-angle problem, and as an advanced quilter you will learn to deal with it. But it will always be better to avoid it if possible, and in the projects in this book, it will always *be* possible.

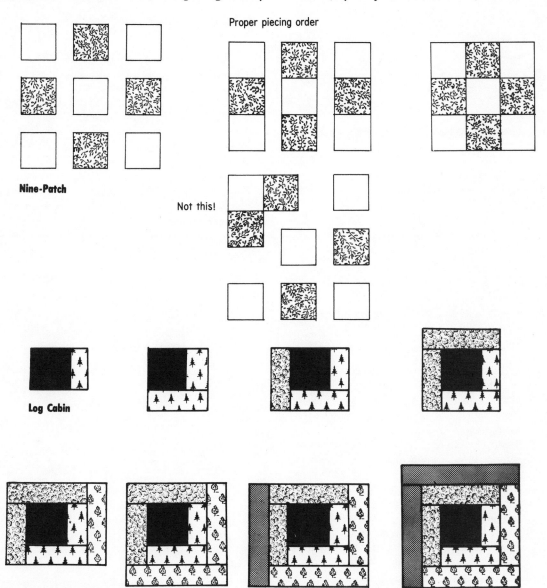

Proper piecing order

Nine-Patch

Not this!

Log Cabin

Stitching the Pieces Together. Use regular polyester thread to stitch pieces together. The color does not need to match exactly. You may use white thread for light fabrics and brown or gray for dark fabrics. Cut a piece of thread about 18″ long and knot one end. You will be stitching such short seams and breaking the thread so often that it would be inefficient and tiring to pull a long thread through every time. Using a shorter thread also minimizes troublesome tangling. Treat the thread with beeswax if you desire.

Maximum stitching strength would be achieved by the use of pure backstitching, but because the needle would have to be pulled completely through the fabric after every stitch, it is not recommended for piecework. The running stitch alone, especially if the stitches are larger, can lead to puckering. Another disadvantage is that if the thread should break during cleaning or usage, an entire seam could come undone.

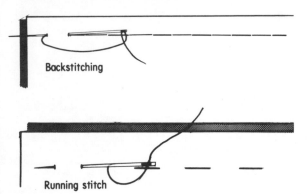

Backstitching

Running stitch

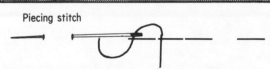

Piecing stitch

Therefore, the pieces should be sewn together using a glorified running stitch, appropriately named the "piecing stitch," which combines the running stitch with an occasional backstitch. Basically, every 3 or 4 running stitches are followed by a single backstitch. With practice you will be able to quickly "run" the 3 or 4 stitches onto the needle all at once. After you have pulled the needle through the fabric completing the set of running stitches, make the backstitch by inserting the needle to the right of the thread as it leaves the fabric. This backstitch becomes the first stitch on the needle as

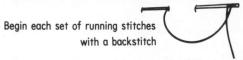

Begin each set of running stitches
with a backstitch

you gather up another set of 3 or 4 running stitches. The piecing stitch is stronger than the simple running stitch due to the frequent backstitching, but doesn't really take any extra time because the backstitch is taken when the needle has already been pulled through the fabric. Counting the stitches on the topside of the fabric only, you should strive for a gauge of 7 to 8 running stitches per inch.

Equally important as strength along the piecing line is strength at the corners where pieces have been joined. To assure accuracy and strength at the corners, use the following method:

1 Insert the needle *exactly* at the corner of the stitching line at the right corner. If you have pinned correctly, the needle will be inserted exactly in the hole made by the right-hand pin.
2 Take one stitch and then backstitch to secure.
3 Take still another backstitch, this time inserting the needle in the center of the first backstitch so as not to put too great a strain on the fabric right at the beginning of the seam.
4 Sew the pieces together using the piecing stitch, with a goal of 8 stitches per inch. Backstitch every 3 or 4 stitches.
5 Secure the left-hand corner with two backstitches, being certain that the needle comes through the fabric exactly at the left-hand pin.
6 Knot the thread by slipping the needle under the backstitches at the corner (be careful not to sew through the fabric as you do this). Pull the needle through to create a loop in the thread. Pass the needle through the loop in the thread and pull it taut to form a knot. Knot again.

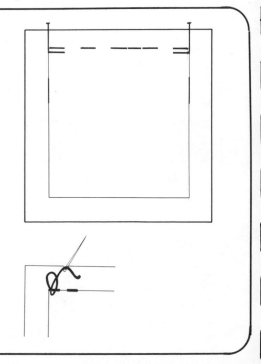

This may seem to be overdoing the backstitching and knotting, but it is wise to do a thorough job now and avoid the tedious quilt-repairing that would be required if this care were not taken at the proper time. Remember: Pieces rarely come apart in the middle of the seam — it is the corners that fall apart first.

By pinning with the two-pin method and stitching with the piecing stitch, you will obtain precision corners and maximum strength. In a very short time this will all become second nature, and you will be able to concentrate on the more creative aspects of quilting.

Joining Rows of Pieces. When one is joining two rows of pieces together, it is possible to join the rows without stitching down the seam allowances. Like the pinning method, this technique can easily be learned and used in all piecing. The rewards are reaped in the final stages of quilting.

Suppose you are joining two rows of two squares each.

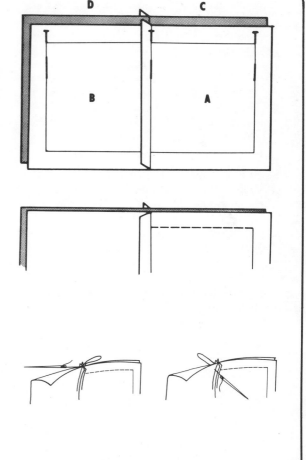

1 With right sides together, pin the right-hand corners of A and C and the left-hand corners of B and D following the two-pin method.
2 Smoothing the seam allowances to the left, pin square A to square C at the left-hand corner of A as though it were the end of the unit being pieced. IMPORTANT: the pin must go precisely into the corner stitching line.
3 Add horizontal pins along the seamline as needed.
4 Begin stitching at the right-hand corner of A, knotting the thread and piecing as you would any two squares (the pins have been omitted from the diagram for the sake of clarity).
5 At the left-hand corner of A, make a backstitch, and knot.
6 Insert the needle through the left-hand corner of A and pull it through the corresponding corner in C.
7 Pass the needle sideways through the seam allowance at the joining corner of C and D and pull the thread through, keeping the seam allowances free.
8 Shift the seam allowance to the right. Now insert the needle through the right corner of D back to the topside of B at its right corner.
9 Pull the needle through, take a stitch as close to the corner as you can (not precisely where the needle passed through to the topside or the stitch will be lost), backstitch, and knot. All the seam allowances should be freestanding.
10 Finish stitching B and D together.

This is a small thing to accomplish (for such a lengthy explanation), but it is worth the extra attention to detail. Notice that you will be able to iron the seam allowances to the right *or* left, depending on the requirements of the design. At times you may choose to iron all the seam allowances away from a light-colored fabric toward a darker fabric through which they will not show. After you have shown yourself that precision piecing with perfectly matched corners is possible, you will be able to eliminate some of the knotting and backstitching in a shortcut method.

In Praise of
Precision

Let us quickly review the things that will determine the quality of your piecework and at the same time remind ourselves of all the time we can save without sacrificing accuracy.

1 The templates in the back of the book are all actual size. No time is needed to graph and enlarge, and no errors will be made.
2 You will mark only the stitching line.
3 You will join pieces exactly from corner to corner using the two-pin method.
4 You will not create frustrations by creating situations that will require right-angle piecing.
5 You will maximize strength and minimize time by using the piecing stitch.
6 You will never stitch down a seam allowance during the piecing process and later discover that the finished project would have been much nicer had the allowances been ironed the other way.

Ironing the Pieced Top. Carefully iron the pieced top on the wrong side. Because the seam allowances are free-standing, you will be able to choose which way they should lie. Usually it is best to press the seam allowances away from light pieces toward the darker pieces. In complicated piecing patterns the pieces may seem to lie in a certain configuration all on their own. For example, in Log Cabin, the seam allowances tend to lie outward toward the edge, forming concentric squares. In Drunkard's Path, the seam allowances will lie naturally away from the curve.

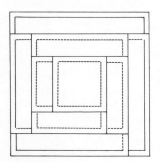

Log Cabin block
Seam allowances lie in concentric squares

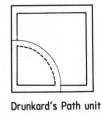

Drunkard's Path unit

Turn the pieced top over and press the topside lightly.

On a small project of lightweight fabrics and uncomplicated design, you may save yourself a session with the hot iron by "finger-pressing" the seam allowances. Simply apply pressure on the seams with your thumb or index finger, moving your hand as if it were the iron.

Choosing, Marking Quilting Designs. It should not be necessary to mark the quilting lines on pieced objects if the largest piece is no larger than 2" square. Quilting is usually done ⅛" to ¼" from the stitching lines. The novice may choose to draw lightly with a washable marker faint guidelines for quilting until she develops a "sixth sense" and can judge the distance routinely with accuracy. If pencil is used, it must be used very lightly — it doesn't wash out.

The old quilts had quilting lines running every 1" or less. This was partially for beauty and partially to keep the old-fashioned batting from bunching up. This is not a problem with polyester batting, and it is not uncommon to see areas as great as 12" square unquilted. Nevertheless, in the projects in this book, spaces greater than 2" will be filled in with some quilting, both to enhance the beauty of the design and to encourage the beginner to set high standards for herself.

Putting the Layers Together. Wadded quilting involves three layers: the quilt top, the wadding or batting, and the quilt backing. The top may be pieced, appliqued, a combination of the two, or a single piece of fabric; the backing may be plain or printed.

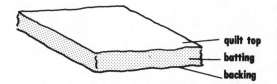

quilt top
batting
backing

The batting provides warmth and bulk. A very thin layer of batting may be used (baby bibs, aprons, and other pieces of clothing) or a very thick layer may be warranted (pot holders, place mats). As a rule, the thicker the batting, the more difficult it will be to quilt the item. It might be wise to sacrifice too much bulk in favor of more beautiful quilting stitches. The old-fashioned quilts were not thick — warmth came from the use of several quilts on one bed. For any hand-quilted project, batting should be ¼" to ½". Batting is a rather difficult thing to measure in regard to thickness, so read the label and hope the manufacturer knows his stuffing. You will soon find that some batting is light and fluffy while another is nearly a thermal weave. Experiment with both if the opportunity arises until you develop a clear preference.

The quilt backing can be plain or fancy. It often happens that the quilting itself is most beautiful when it is seen from the back of the quilt where the colors and designs of the top don't overwhelm its simplicity. A simple white or off-white quilt backing is usually ideal, although many people prefer to use a printed fabric, thereby making the quilt "reversible." For pillow tops and other small projects in which the backing is completely hidden, it will not matter at all what fabric is used. A loosely woven fabric will give the beginner her best chance for success. If the 80″-88″ wide muslin quilt backing is available to you, by all means invest in a yard to be used for pillows and other small projects. It is extremely economical and is a dream to quilt through. A word of caution: Don't listen to people who tell you to buy a permanent-pressed sheet for your backing, on a quilt or otherwise. The finish is often impenetrable by the average quilter and the thread count (180 threads per inch) is too great!

The quilting stitch is a means of securing the layers together. Through the years the stitching has become far more than functional and enlivens the surface texture of the quilt top with a beauty of its own.

Note: If the project is small (less than 18″ square), the quilt batting and backing should always be cut a generous 2″ to 3″ larger on all sides than the finished top. Up to 6″ should be allowed on larger projects. This excess is sometimes "taken up" as the top is stretched flat during quilting.

It will not be difficult to center the layers for a small quilted project. Simply lay the quilt backing (right-side down if there is one) on a table. Lay the batting on top of it. Then lay the pieced top in the middle of the others, evenly distributing the excess on all 4 sides. For a project larger than 36″, it takes only a minute to "quarter and center" the layers as described in the information on traditional frame quilting.

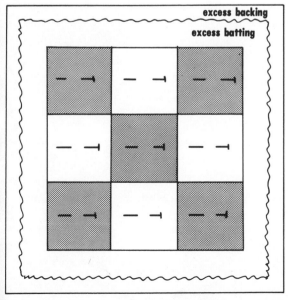

excess backing
excess batting

Pinning and/or Basting. Smooth the 3 layers to remove lumps and wrinkles. Any lump or crease not eliminated now will remain in the finished product.

If the project is small, or if a chair-side frame is to be used, pin-baste the 3 layers together. Pin-baste means to temporarily hold the layers together with pins instead of running a long basting stitch through the layers and then removing the pins. Begin at the center and pin every 2″ to 3″, being certain that the quilt top is not

distorted in any way. You may choose to actually baste the layers together and remove all the pins. This would be wise if the project exceeds 24″ square, or if it will be moved around for quite a long time, or if young children seem to enjoy participating in your activities more than you like. In any of these cases, baste through all the thicknesses in rows radiating from the center. Do not use black thread for basting — it leaves a telltale residue very unbecoming to most quilting projects. Some reds have the same nasty habit.

Pins are now rustproof and there is really no danger in leaving the pins in the fabric for an extended period of time.

On large projects it will be difficult to slip your left hand under the fabric to facilitate pinning. Learn to pin one-handed, pushing against the protected tabletop or floor, checking that each pin is free of the tablecloth or rug by lifting the quilt slightly off the surface before securing the pin.

When the layers are secured together, turn the project over to examine the quilt backing for wrinkles. Double-check that the backing does indeed reach the farthest edges of the batting. Alas, experienced quilters (who should have known better) have been known to quilt merrily along with no backing beneath the batting to secure the stitches.

Pin-basting the layers together

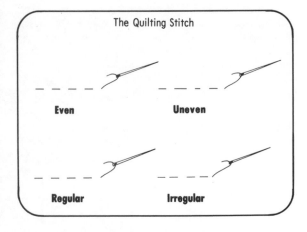

The Quilting Stitch

Even · Uneven

Regular · Irregular

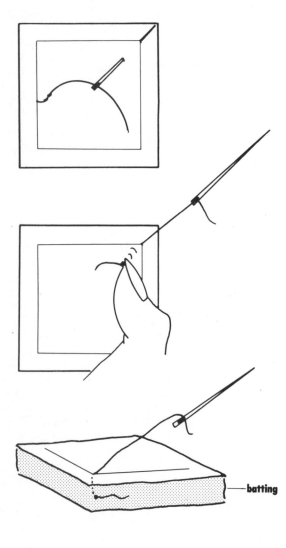

batting

IMPORTANT! *Do not trim the excess batting or backing until the quilting is actually finished.* Quilting sometimes changes the tensions on the layers and more of the batting will be drawn in. This is particularly noticeable with beginners. If the quilting is begun at the center and worked out toward the edges, the pins can be adjusted and more of the batting allowed between the top and backing. This is not usually a major problem, but it pays to be careful.

The Quilting Stitch. Use quilting thread and a size 7 or 8 quilting needle ("between"). The stitching is done in small, regular stitches which must go through all thicknesses. The *evenness* (the uniform size of the stitches) and the *regularity* (the uniform distance between each stitch) are the two most important qualities of good quilting. The number of stitches per inch and proper tension are also important. The tension of the stitches creates the puffed appearance of the well done quilt.

Burying the Knot and Quilting. Thread the needle with 18″ to 24″ of quilting thread. Knot one end of the thread. Insert the needle in the top of the quilt about an inch from the desired beginning of the quilting line. *Do not go through all of the thicknesses* — keep the needle above the batting. Drawing the needle between the top and the batting, bring the point of the needle to the top of the fabric at the desired beginning of the quilting line. Pull the needle through. Use your left thumbnail to pull against the fabric at the knot (do not pull against the knot itself) as you pull the needle toward the right with your right hand. The knot should slip through the top layer. Pull the thread taut so that the knot is now directly under the beginning of the quilting line and does not show on the backside of the quilt. This process is called "burying the knot" and is really quite simple. Always begin in this manner.

With your left hand, gather up the layers to the left of the beginning of the quilting. Use your left index finger and thumb to pinch the layers together just to the left of the buried knot. Push the needle vertically down through all the layers of the quilt until your left index fingernail feels the point of the needle against it. Do not push the needle all the way through quite yet. Push up against the needle with the left index fingernail and guide the needle back into the quilt backing. Pivoting your right wrist, bring the needle back to the top of the fabric and pull it through. Stitch #1 has been completed. Continue in this manner, 1 stitch at a time, keeping the stitches as small and even as possible. As you become more skilled, you will find that you are able to run 3 or 4 stitches onto the needle at one time and pull the thread through all of them simultaneously.

There are no backstitches in quilting. Remember to stitch vertically — this helps create the proper tension.

How small should the stitches be? For a beginner, 6 or 7 stitches is a realistic goal, counting only the stitches that appear on the top. An ultimate goal might be 10 stitches per inch. For years I'd been intimidated by boasts of oldtime quilters who manage 20 stitches per inch. Then I discovered that some of these quilters quilted with the backstitch. The space between our stitches counted as a separate stitch for them. If you could manage 10 of *our* stitches per inch, you would be considered extremely talented (and a little bit crazy!).

You may find that while you manage 6 or 7 stitches per inch quite easily, it takes a good deal of concentration to squeeze in 2 more stitches. Therefore, you would probably be better off sticking with the lower stitch count than playing havoc with the evenness and regularity by pinching in 2 more stitches. As you quilt, simply think small and do your best.

What is proper in terms of tension? That is hard to describe. The quilt top should be slightly depressed at the quilting lines. Too little tension will cause the lack of this depression. To check for the problem, slide a pin under a stitch in the middle of a quilted row. Pull upwards on the stitch. There should be no slack. If there is, begin at the beginning of the row and work the slack toward the loose end of the thread to eliminate the excess. You will need to pull harder on the thread after each few quilting stitches. If, instead, the piece is bunching up, ease up on the tension. This, too, comes with practice.

Never, ever, backstitch in the quilting process. The tension is never the same as the other stitches. The backstitch tends to "bead up" and ruin the otherwise beautiful quilting.

Ending the Quilting Thread. The fewer beginnings and endings of quilting thread in a project, the stronger the quilting, it is said. Oftentimes, one will notice backstitching where quilting threads were started and ended. Unless these stitches are few and neatly done, they will detract from the overall beauty of the quilting.

This!

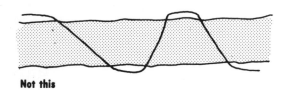

Not this

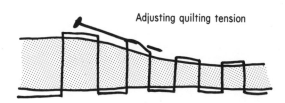

Adjusting quilting tension

So, just as you "bury the knot" at the beginning of a quilting thread, you will bury it at its end. With 2" to 4" of thread remaining in the needle, make a loop of thread near the fabric. Draw the needle through it, but do not pull it taut. Insert the point of the needle back into the loop and press the point against the fabric where the next stitch would be taken. Begin to tighten the loop, pulling the thread with the left hand, forming a knot with the point of the needle through its middle. As the left hand tightens the knot, the right hand controls the formation of the knot about a stitch-length of thread from the point at which the thread left the quilt top. Pull the needle out of the knot. Insert the needle where the next stitch would be, but stay between the layers (above the batting). Bring the needle back to the top of the fabric about 1" away, in a pieced seam, if possible. Pull the needle through. Pulling the needle with the left hand, use the right thumbnail to work the knot into the fabric. This is the reverse of burying the knot at the beginning. Pull the thread taut to gather the quilt top slightly and trim the thread close to the fabric. As you smooth the fabric, the end of the thread will be pulled inside the layers.

If there happens to be a seam nearby, you may hide a few tiny backstitches *in the seam* for extra security. How well you secure the beginning and ending of each quilting thread will determine how much wear and how many washings your quilted project will endure.

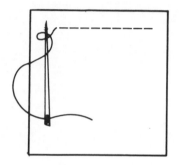
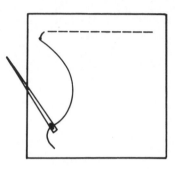

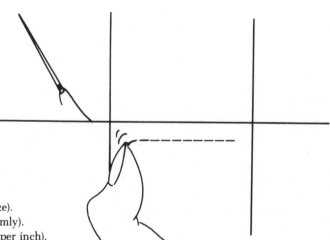

Fundamentals of Quality Quilting

1 Evenness of stitches (all the same size).
2 Regularity of stitches (spaced uniformly).
3 Length of stitch (number of stitches per inch).
4 Tension.
5 Uniformity of quilting design. (Are the lines straight and a uniform distance from the pieces' seams?)
6 Lack of knots and backstitches.
7 Appearance of stitches on the backing.

Chapter 2/Piecing Squares

Simple Nine-Patch

Beginning with a conveniently sized piece and an easy pattern, you will choose one of two available fabric combinations. The project will be pieced, quilted, and completed as either a hot pad, wall decoration, mini-pillow, or tooth-fairy pillow.

6″ Finished Hot Pad or Pillow

Materials

1/4 yd. Fabric A, 44/45″ wide
1/4 yd. Fabric B, 44/45″ wide
10″ square quilt backing
10″ square quilt batting
9″ square pillow or hot pad backing (Fabric A or B)
Polyester filling for pillows or layers of quilt batting for
   hot pad — two 10″ squares

Optional

3/4 yd. lace or eyelet for pillows
1/8 yd. 44/45″ Fabric A or B for ruffle for pillow

Template Cutting. Cut the 2″ square template from the book. Following the general instructions, make a cardboard template. Check the accuracy of your template.

Marking and Cutting the Fabric

Fabric A	5 squares
Fabric B	5 squares

Squares are easy to mark on the fabric because the sides of the template fall naturally into line with the grain of the fabric (straight or cross), and because no thought is required to use the fabric efficiently.

Remember that the lines you have drawn are *stitching lines.* DO NOT CUT ON THE LINES.

Choosing the Fabric Combination. Notice that you were instructed to cut 10 squares for a nine-patch pillow. This is simply because it is useful for the beginner to experiment at an early stage with color and fabric combinations. Using 9 of the 10 squares, you will be able to create 2 different combinations. Experiment by arranging the squares on the table and make a choice.

If you feel you do not have a knack for selecting colors and combining prints, use this technique often to reinforce your initial decisions. Cutting out lots of extra pieces from all the potential fabrics, most of which will be rejected, may seem unbearably tedious if the project

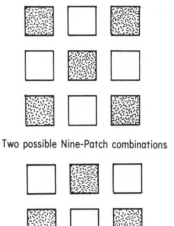

Two possible Nine-Patch combinations

is a simple pillow. However, the lesson learned will be of great value when the end product is a quilt of a thousand pieces.

Piecing. Using colored thread, begin piecing the left-hand row of squares together, starting at the top. *Stitch on the line!* After you have joined 3 rows of 3 squares each, join the rows together.

Finger-Pressing. If the stitching is straight and not too tight, it is not usually necessary to iron a small pieced project. Instead, lay the pieced top on a table right-side down and press the seam allowances to one side or the other with your index finger. You are free to decide which way to press the seam allowances based on the color of the pieces or the design of the pattern.

Assembling the Layers. If finger-pressing does not satisfy you, iron the pieced top on both the wrong and right sides. Use a light touch.

Because the quilt backing will not be visible in this project, it really hasn't a right or wrong side. Layer the pieced top, batting, and quilt backing, with the excess batting and backing evenly distributed on all 4 sides of the pieced top. Pin or baste the layers together.

Quilting. On a small project which is being quilted without a frame, it is always best to begin quilting in the middle and to work toward the edges. Because the quilt backing will not show on the finished product, it is not imperative that the quilting knots be buried. One should, however, begin attempting the technique. The quilting stitches should form perpendicular lines at the corners. After the first square is quilted, slip the needle "between the layers" with the needle point coming to the surface of the pieced top exactly in the corner of the quilting line of the neighboring square. Continue quilting.

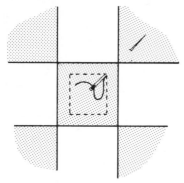

The outer edges present a new problem. It is easy to determine the quilting line $^{1}/_{8}''$ inside the seams on the center square, but it is easy to make an error on the outermost edges. Do not quilt $^{1}/_{8}''$ from the outer edge. *Remember that the quilting must be $^{1}/_{8}''$ inside the stitching line.* Mark the stitching line with horizontal pins; then quilt $^{1}/_{8}''$ inside the imaginary lines made by the pins.

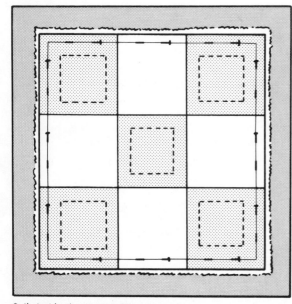

Quilt inside the pins marking piecing lines

Trim all of the layers $^{1}/_{4}''$ larger than the outer seamlines.

Completion As a Hot Pad — Folded Miter. Pillow backing usually refers to the fabric actually on the back of the pillow. It is simply a part of pillow construction and is not involved in actual quilting. Because the beginner's quilting is not yet ready for public inspection, a "pillow backing" is going to be added to the quilted top for this hot pad, as well.

Lay the quilted top upon the 2 additional squares of batting. Trim any excess from these layers so that the top and batting layers are all alike. Lay the pillow backing fabric right side down on the table. Center the quilt top and battings on the backing, right sides up. Trim the pillow backing to ¾" larger than the quilt top on all 4 sides.

Pin or baste the layers together. Fold the excess pillow backing in half along one edge, so that the cut edge lies alongside the layers of batting. Bring this folded edge up over the sides of the batting and lay it carefully along the outer seamlines of the pieced top. Pin in place.

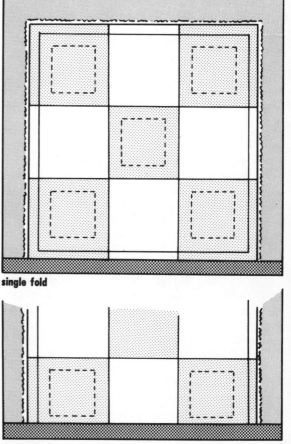

single fold

double fold

To miter the next side, make the first fold on that side as you did the first fold on the other side; that is, fold the excess pillow backing in half so that the cut edge lies along the edge of the batting. At the corner where the 2 sides meet, bring point A to point C. Then make the second fold in the pillow backing on the second side. There should be a neat 45-degree angle at the junction of the 2 sides. Pin carefully.

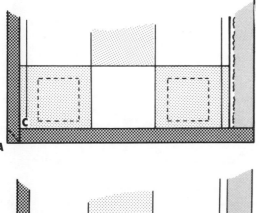

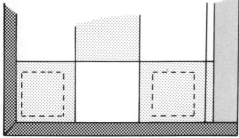

Complete the folding and mitering process. Stitch the backing in place using the blindstitch. After you have finished the nine-patch as a hot pad, sew a plastic ring on the back for hanging.

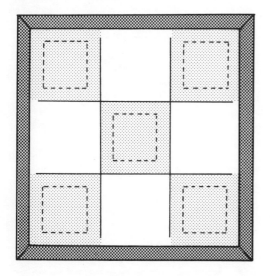

Wall Decoration. You may instead choose to frame the item. Make 2 more nine-patches of a coordinating fabric scheme and decorate a small corner of your kitchen with your artwork.

Tooth-Fairy Pillow. This is for the 5-year-olds on your gift list. The extra square you cut will be the pocket on the back of the pillow for the fairy's quarter.

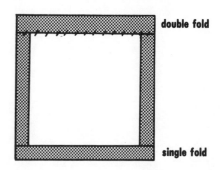

Turn under the seam allowance on all 4 sides of the square. On 1 side, fold under the raw edge and hem it in place. Pin the pocket to the center of the pillow backing. Determine the center by quartering the pillow backing and the pocket. Line up the division markings. Carefully blindstitch the pocket to the pillow on 3 sides, or stitch the pocket on using the machine.

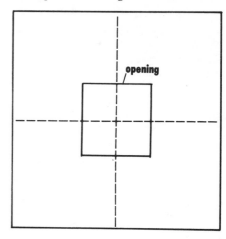

Join the pillow backing according to the basic pillow instructions.

Mini-Pillow. This little pillow can be used as a doll pillow for a youngster, as a jumbo pincushion for yourself, or as a gift for a college girl for her sorority or fraternity pin.

Full-length instructions are included here to cover the many different alternatives for pillow making.

The Basic Pillow. Before you trim any excess batting or backing, baste, by hand or machine, a line around the quilted top which designates the outer seamlines of the pieces. This is most easily done from the topside.

Trim the batting and backing a uniform distance from the basting line on all sides. A ½″ seam allowance is comfortable. It does not matter that the seam allowances on the pieces are less than the ½″.

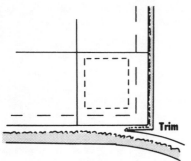

If no ruffles, lace, or piping are to be added, simply lay the pillow backing and quilted pillow top together, right sides together. Pin them together, with the pins perpendicular to the edges of the pillow. This will enable you to sew over the pins with the sewing machine. With the quilt backing facing you, stitch around the pillow, leaving an opening for turning. You should be able to follow your basting line, stitching slightly inside it, so that the thread will not show on the finished pillow.

To leave the opening for stuffing at the most advantageous spot, begin stitching an inch or 2 from one corner. Stitch to the corner, around the other 3 sides, turn the fourth corner, and stitch to within 4″ of the beginning. Backstitch at the beginning and end. A 4″ to 6″ opening is ideal — less than 4″ will not allow you to insert your hand for easier stuffing.

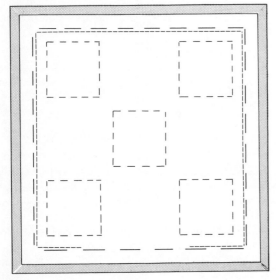

Seamstresses all recommend cutting the corners slightly as you stitch the pillow. Angling the last ⅛″ on a side actually creates a sharper point on the finished pillow.

Do not turn the pillow until you have read the section on reinforcing the pillow backing.

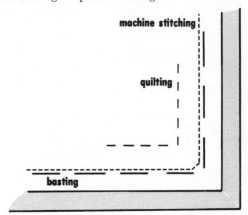

Lace, Eyelet, and Ready-made Piping. Pin the lace, pre-gathered eyelet, or piping to the right side of the quilted top, laying the stitching line of the decorative edging directly on the basted line on the quilted top. The seam allowance of the fancy edging should lie against the seam allowance of the pieced top, with the pretty edge toward the center. Do not begin the edging at the corner of the pillow.

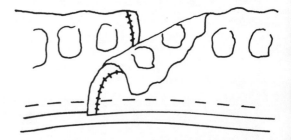

On lace or eyelet, fold under ¼″ hems on both ends of the edging. You may need to stitch the hems carefully to prevent fraying. Then overlap the 2 ends by ½″ as you pin the edging in place. Do not begin and end the lace on the same side which will have the opening for turning the pillow inside-out.

For a ready-made piping edging, conceal the ends by easing the ends of the piping into the seams after they have overlapped ½″.

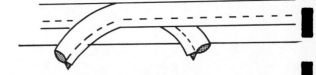

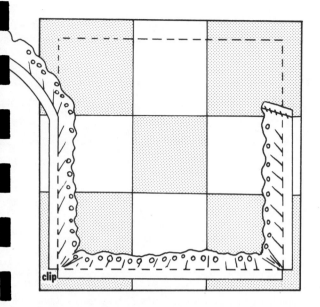

On all edgings, allow excess at the corners, clipping the seam allowance to facilitate the turn.

To be safe, run a quick machine-basting line along the seamline on the edging. Turn the pieced top over. On the backside, the basting threads should coincide. Then pin the pretty edge of the edging to the quilted top to keep it from being caught in the seam as the pillow backing is joined. This preventive pinning is especially important at the corners.

Lay the pillow backing on the quilted top, right sides together. Pin. Stitch them together, using the basting line on the quilt backing as a guide. Stitch inside the basting line. Leave an ample opening for turning and stuffing.

Read the section for reinforcing the pillow backing before you turn the pillow.

Ruffles. A double-thickness ruffle is most attractive because it has no wrong side. To determine how much fabric to cut, measure the perimeter of the pillow (the distance around it). Allow 1½ to 2 times that distance for the total length of the ruffle. For the 6″ mini-pillow, 36″ should suffice. Determine the desired width of the finished ruffle. For the mini-pillow, 1½″ should be adequate. Multiply the width by 2 and add seam allowances of ¼″ to ½″ on each side. With ½″ seam allowances, the total for the mini-pillow should be 4″.

Length of ruffle = perimeter of pillow x 1½

Width of ruffle = (desired width + seam allowance) x 2

Cut the strip of fabric and piece it, if necessary, to obtain the proper length. With right sides together, sew the short ends of the strip together, forming a ring. With the seam on the inside, fold the fabric in half lengthwise to form the 2″ ruffle, 2 layers thick, wrong sides together.

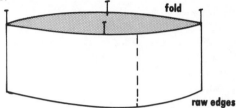

Run a gathering thread ½″ from the raw edge. Divide the ruffle into quarters, marking each division with a pin. Mark the midpoint of each of the 4 sides of the quilted top. Match the pins in the ruffle to the pins in the quilted top and secure it in place. Allowing a generous excess at the corners, pin the ruffle to the quilted top, matching the gathering thread of the ruffle to the basting line on the quilted top. Machine-baste.

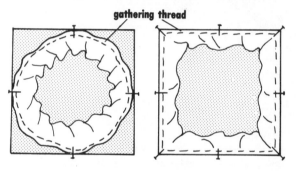

To prevent the ruffle from being caught in the seam when the top and back of the pillow are joined, pin along the folded edge of the ruffle every 2″ to 3″ and at the corners. Stitch 3 sides as instructed under the basic pillow.

Lace or Eyelet and Ruffle Edgings. The effect of the double edging is very professional. It is important that the ruffle extends beyond the lace or eyelet; how *much* it should extend depends upon the size of the pillow and the width of the lace or eyelet.

Treat the 2 edgings as individual units. First apply the eyelet or lace. Baste. Then gather and pin on the ruffle. Though a chore, basting the ruffle on will assure proper placement. Check the quilt backing—do the basting lines coincide?

Take great care to pin the edging and ruffle away from the seam allowances at the corners. Join the pillow backing as instructed.

Double Ruffles. A second, narrower ruffle of a contrasting fabric creates a "framing" effect just as a border does. The narrow ruffle should be ½" to 1" less than the finished width of the wide ruffle. To obtain a ruffle 1" narrower, cut the fabric 2" narrower than the width of the wide ruffle. The lengths of the 2 ruffles should be the same.

Join the ends of each ruffle individually and iron them in half lengthwise. Then lay the raw edges together and gather the ruffles as 1 unit. Pin and stitch the double ruffle as a single unit.

Reinforcing the Pillow Backing. Partly due to the type of filling, and partly due to the thinness of the pillow backing fabric, the backs of most pillows are slightly lumpy. A quick and easy method to eliminate the problem is worthy of mention.

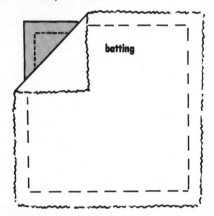

Cut a piece of quilt batting 1" larger on all sides than the finished top will be. Accuracy is not critical—more than 1" will be fine. After the quilt top and pillow backing have been joined on 3 sides, lay the pillow down, pillow backing side up. Center the batting upon it, evenly distributing the excess. Using long basting stitches, and without pins if you are able, baste the batting to the seam allowance of the pillow backing on all 4 sides, along the opening as well. Baste as closely as possible to the seam joining the top and the backing. Easy, wasn't it!

Finishing the Pillow—All Varieties. Carefully clip the corners from the quilted top and any edgings. Do not clip the pillow backing or extra batting layer.

Turn the pillow right side out, mindful of all the pins. Remove all of the pins from the pillow.

Using the eraser end of a pencil, gently push the corners out. The excess batting will roll over along the seam and fold back on itself at the corners, forming a "shoulder pad" of stuffing. This extra padding is desirable because it supports what would otherwise be saggy corners.

Keeping the extra batting layer against the pillow backing, stuff the pillow. Force handfuls into the corner areas. Stuff the pillow to your liking. Pin the opening closed and mash the pillow, trying flatten it. Add more stuffing if necessary. You may choose to baste the opening shut temporarily. Using the pillow for a day or two should settle the filling. Continue to add stuffing to suit yourself.

To permanently close the pillow, fold under the pillow backing along the seamline. Blindstitch the pillow backing to the seamline on the quilted top.

The "Any Fool Can Do It" Pillow for Non-Seamstresses

It occasionally happens that someone who loves quilting either has no sewing machine or has no self-confidence in her pillow-making. For this person, a simple method is recommended. The pillow will not be fancy, but it will display a fine job of piecing and quilting.

Finish the quilted pillow top. Baste a line on the outer edge to designate the finished seamline. Trim the excess batting and backing ½" larger than the finished seamline. Cut an extra piece of batting precisely this size.

Lay the quilt top on the fabric for the pillow backing. Cut a pillow backing 1" larger on all sides than the trimmed batting and backing. Stack the layers as follows:

1 Pillow backing, right side down.
2 Loose piece of batting.
3 Quilted pillow top, right side up.

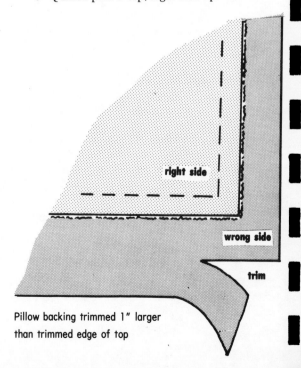

Pillow backing trimmed 1" larger than trimmed edge of top

Join the top and backing along the basting line, leaving an opening for stuffing. The stitches must be neat and as small as possible. They will show on the pillow backing. Stuff the pillow and stitch the opening closed. Fold and miter the seam allowance of the pillow backing according to the instructions for the nine-patch hot pad. Blindstitch the pillow backing to the quilted top. The fabric-covered seam allowances form a piping effect around the pillow.

The results are really quite satisfactory considering the easy method. No longer is there an excuse for unfinished pillow tops!

If this method doesn't suit you, but you cannot manage the more sophisticated versions, hire someone to make your pillows for you. A quilter is not necessarily a pillow-maker. Do what you enjoy and pay someone else to worry about the rest.

Note: If polyester batting and stuffing have been used, the pillow will be machine-washable and dryable. Dry thoroughly at a low heat setting. Cotton-filled pillows are not washable, and, because drying is difficult, mildew may result.

Sunshine and Shadow

The Amish quilters of America have made a substantial contribution to our heritage. Several patterns, worked in solid-colored fabrics, are attributed to them. One of these is Sunshine and Shadow or Trip Around the World. Both are made of rows of squares. The placement of the fabrics seems to determine the pattern name.

If the colors begin with one hue at the center and work in rows through the color wheel (or a part thereof), returning to the original hue, it is a Trip Around the World. If, instead, the fabrics vary in shade or brightness within a hue family, it may be called Sunshine and Shadow. Actually, you will readily find either color display under either name. The squares are often tipped sideways to form concentric diamonds of color.

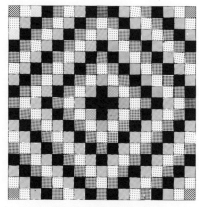

Trip Around the World

To simplify matters, a small section, perhaps from a corner of the design, can be pieced and quilted as a pillow. The opportunity to experiment with color should be taken. The Amish used solid-colored fabrics. You may, however, choose to use prints.

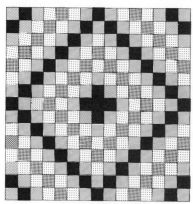

Sunshine and Shadow

10″ Pillow

Materials

½ yd. Fabric A, 44/45″ wide, for pieces, pillow backing and ruffle (darkest fabric)

⅛ yd. Fabric B, 44/45″ wide for pieces (middle fabric)

⅛ yd. Fabric C, 44/45″ wide for pieces (lightest or most eye-catching fabric)

14″ quilt batting

14″ quilt backing

Polyester filling

Template. Use the 2″ square template to mark the fabric according to the usual method.

Number of Pieces Required

Fabric A	7 squares
Fabric B	12 squares
Fabric C	6 squares
Total	25 squares

Cutting. Cut the pieces from Fabric A in such a way as to leave a straight width for ruffles and a square large enough for the pillow backing. Cut the pieces from B and C.

Stacking and Threading. Arrange the pieces on a table. Beginning with the lower left square, stack the 5 pieces in row 1 so that the upper left-hand square is on top. Stack row 2, bottom to top. Stack all 5 rows. Now stack the rows, with the right-hand row on the bottom.

You will be able to piece all of the squares into rows and the rows together without referring to a diagram.

Piecing. Using the same methods described for the simple nine-patch, piece the squares into rows and join rows. Iron the pieced top.

Quilting. Stack the 3 layers, centering the pieced top on the batting and backing. Quilt diagonal lines through the center of each fabric row. Add additional quilting lines if you desire.

Finish As a Ruffled Pillow.

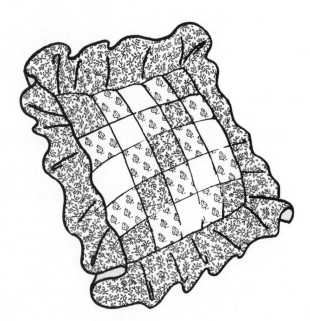

Problem-Solving

1 If there is a hole between the pieces where 4 squares join, pay more careful attention to pinning as rows are joined. You must stitch the end of 1 square exactly to the end of the square joining it.

2 If you have noticed that your piecing stitches do not follow the piecing line on the square underneath, do not despair. A deviation of 1/16″ along the line is tolerable *if the beginning and ending match exactly.* If the deviation is greater, remove the stitching. Add 2 horizontal pins along the seam to prevent the problem in the future.

3 If you find that dark seam allowances are showing through the pieced top, carefully trim the dark seam allowances so that they are concealed by wider, light-colored seam allowances. This problem can be eliminated quite simply. As you mark the pieces on light fabric, leave larger seam allowances than you do on dark fabrics. Automatically the problem will be resolved.

4 Your finished quilt top should be 10″ square (9¾″ to 10¼″ is acceptable for beginners). Deviation in size can be due to incorrect piecing, improper marking, or an inaccurate template. Try to eliminate problems in the future.

Chapter 3/Piecing Triangles Borders and Cording

This lesson will apply marking and piecing techniques to triangles. Two patterns are included in this chapter. The beginner must complete one or the other. Neither is more difficult. One simply has more pieces, and therefore will require more time.

In addition to mastering the technique of piecing triangles, the beginner will experiment with the addition of borders. The lesson teaches both the techniques in borders and the artistic effect. Bias binding for piping and cording is covered in detail.

Fabric A

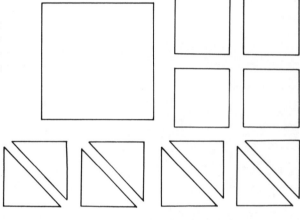

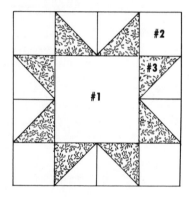

Simple Star

11″ Finished size (without borders)

Fabric B

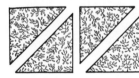

Materials

½ yd. Fabric A, 44/45″ wide for light pieces in diagrams (optional border and pillow backing)

½ yd. Fabric B, 44/45″ wide for dark pieces in diagram (optional border and pillow backing)

15″ square quilt batting (does not include borders)

15″ square quilt backing (does not include borders)

Polyester filling

2 yds. cording, 15/64″ or 7/23″, polyester

Templates. Cut out the paper templates from the book. Except for the #3 triangle, it should not be necessary to cut templates from cardboard.

Number of Pieces Required

Fabric A	1 piece	#1
	4 pieces	#2
	8 pieces	#3
Fabric B	8 pieces	#3
Total	21 pieces	

Marking the Fabric and Cutting. Do not cut borders or pillow backing until the entire unit has been pieced. If your marking and piecing are not exactly accurate, your borders could be either too big or too small. If the pieces in the top are neatly joined, the accuracy of the size is not important. Simply cut the borders to the size you require.

This is the last time specific layout instructions will be given. After this, you will have to rely on your own good judgment.

Piecing. Study the diagram to decide what will be the easiest approach to piecing. *Hint:* What is the difference between the four squares?

There is no difference! Therefore, it is recommended that you sew the 8A triangles to the 8B triangles to form 8 AB squares *first*. Then rotate each AB square as necessary to piece it into the pattern.

Pay particular attention to the piecing order of the central portion of the star.

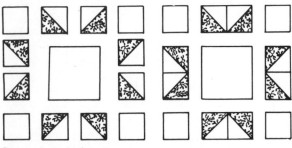

Proper piecing order

Advanced Techniques

Stacking and Threading. Stack and thread the four #2 squares with the #1 square. Stack and thread the #3 triangles in a second pile, alternating the A and B fabrics. Piece the triangles into squares, taking each triangle from the stack in order.

The One-Pin Method. If you have proved to yourself that corners *can* match, you are ready for a simplified pinning method.

In short, as you pin two pieces, pin only the left-hand edge. After it is properly aligned, use the point of the threaded needle to bring the right-hand edge into line. Pinch the fabric immediately to the left of the needle between the thumb and index finger of the left hand to hold it secure. Take one stitch. After you have back-stitched, the beginning will be properly secured and aligned.

Keeping Seam Allowances Freestanding. In the elementary method, you passed the needle through to the back from A to C, through the back seam allowances to D, and then through to the top again to B. If there have been no gaps in your piecing, you may use a simplified method. When you reach the junction of square A and square B, simply slide the needle through to the beginning of square B. Eliminating the steps to squares C and D will save time.

If ever you notice gaps reappearing in your piecing, correct the problem by returning to the long method.

Borders. You have been instructed to buy sufficient fabric for borders and pillow backing from both Fabric A and Fabric B. This will enable you to study the effect of different borders on a quilt top. Fold both Fabrics A and B into 15″ squares. Study the appearance of the pieced top on both. Examine the effect of wide or narrow borders by moving the pieced top closer to a corner of the fabric.

Determine which fabric you prefer and select a width for your borders.

Measure the sides of the pieced top. If the sides are not all the same (shame on you!), use the largest number in your planning. Slight deviations can be eased in over the length of the entire border.

Simple Borders. Cut 2 borders the length of the side and the width you have selected, adding seam allowances. Cut 2 more borders the length of a side plus twice the width. Use your 18″ ruler to mark the stitching line, or make templates.

Join the borders according to the diagram, avoiding a right-angle piecing situation.

Mitered Borders. If you would like to miter the corners of your borders and enjoy a challenge, make a border template. All 4 borders will be cut from the same template.

Let "L" represent the length of 1 side. Let "W" represent the width of your borders. Cut a template from cardboard that is L + 2W long. It should be W in width. At both ends of the template, mark the squares that have W as a side. Draw diagonals according to the diagram and trim away the 2 triangles. This is your finished template.

width　　　　　　　length　　　　　　　width

Cut 4 borders, using this template in the usual manner, adding seam allowances.

Join the first border, matching the short edge exactly to the side of the pieced top. Pin a second border to the joined border along the mitered corner. Piece the borders together. At the intersection of the 2 borders and the corner of the pieced top, pivot to join the border to the top. Pin and stitch the second border to the side of the pieced top. Join the other 2 borders.

This requires piecing a 45-degree angle, which is not terribly difficult. The professional finish is well worth the trouble.

Quilting. Cut the quilt backing and batting 2″ larger than the top and borders on all sides.

Quilt ⅛″ inside the seams on either Fabric A pieces or Fabric B pieces, or both. The large square in the center is too large to leave unquilted. In washable marker, or *very light* pencil, draw a quilting design of your choosing. (See Appendix II: Quilting Designs) Quilt along the borders as usual.

Bias Binding and Cording. Make the bias according to the instructions (see Appendix I). Preshrink the cording, knotting the ends to prevent raveling.

Cut lengths of bias and cording 5″ longer than the perimeter of the pillow plus borders. Fold the bias over the cording, matching the raw edges. Stitch the cording into place, very loosely, using the zipper foot. If you stitch the cording too tightly at this point, it will be difficult to conceal the stitching later.

Baste the seamline on the quilted top as you have on the other pillows. Lay the cording along this line, extending the rolled edge toward the center of the quilted top. Carefully turn the corners, clipping the seam allowance of the bias binding as necessary. Pin in place.

splice ends of cording

To join the ends of the cording nicely, you will have to join both the bias binding and the cording itself. Open the seam encasing the cording at both ends. Fold under the raw edge on 1 end. Trim the other end so that it overlaps about ½″. Trim the ends of the cording so that they overlap about 1″, preferably slightly away from the bias junction. Untwine both ends of the cording where they overlap. Splice the cording by cutting away half of the ply on each end. Twist the remaining ply together and whipstitch the 1″ area of splicing. Fold the bias back over the cording and baste it through all the layers.

Using the zipper foot, stitch just inside the basting thread on the quilt backing. Finish the pillow, leaving the opening for turning at the opposite end of the pillow.

Fabric cording can be used alone or with other decorative edgings. Always apply the cording first. Check its placement by basting. Then add the other edgings.

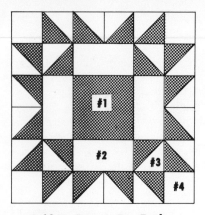

Robbing Peter to Pay Paul

9″ Finished size (without borders)

Materials

½ yd. Fabric A, 44/45″ wide for dark pieces, pillow backing, and borders (optional)

¼ yd. Fabric B, 44/45″ wide for light pieces and borders (optional)

13″ quilt backing (does not include borders)

13″ quilt batting (does not include borders)

Polyester filling

Decorative edgings (optional)

Number of Pieces Required

Fabric A	1 piece #1
	20 pieces #3
Fabric B	4 pieces #2
	20 pieces #3
	4 pieces #4
Total	49 pieces

Cutting. Do not cut the border strips and pillow backing, quilt backing, and batting until you know the size of the pieced top.

Piecing. Piecing for this project is the same as for Simple Star, except that 5 vertical rows will be pieced and then joined.

Adding Borders. Experiment with both Fabric A and B as border fabrics. Cut and join borders using the simple or mitered method.

Quilting. Quilt inside the A pieces or B pieces, ⅛″ from the seamlines. Quilting on the borders is optional. Quilt concentric squares inside piece #1, or create your own design.

Finish As a Pillow.

Problem-Solving

The most common problem with both of these patterns is that little gaps appear in the piecing where 2 pairs of triangles join a long, unpieced seam. This occurs in the center, double-width row in both Simple Star and Robbing Peter to Pay Paul. The solution is simple. The example is Simple Star.

1 Join Fabric A and Fabric B triangles together to form AB squares.

Join the AB squares together, matching two corners exactly.

2 With the AB squares facing you, pin the squares to the #1 square, matching the right and left corners exactly.

3 Insert a vertical pin at the center of seam b, making certain that the pin centers the seamlines on the #1 square.

4 If there is any easing to be done, it should be evenly divided between the 2 squares.

5 Add horizontal pins along the piecing lines.

6 Piece from a to b. Backstitch at b.

7 Slide the needle through the seam allowance to c.

8 Insert the needle at c in preparation for the first stitch, and check the back of the fabric to see where the needle is coming through.

9 On the #1 square, the needle must poke through exactly where the last backstitch at b ended. Tipping the fabric so you can see the #1 square, reinsert the needle to the proper place.

10 When you find the proper place to stitch, backstitch, and then finish the seam.

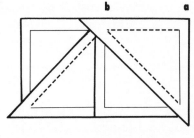

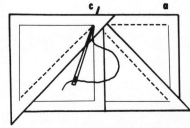

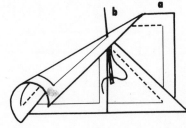

It is the angle at which the needle enters the fabric which causes or eliminates this gap. This method will apply whenever a row of pieces is joining a solid piece of fabric.

Use this technique to successfully join borders to the pieced top, as well.

UNIT II
Chapter 4 / Piecing Hexagons

This pattern is a one-patch — it has only one pattern piece. Its simplicity does not restrict its beauty due to the wide variety of designs in which the pieces can be combined.

Hexagons can be sewn together in concentric rings to form a mosaic tile pattern that becomes a very striking quilt. It is not necessary to actually piece the quilt in circles — one would have quite a lapful after the first few rows. By using the same arranging and stacking techniques which we used in Sunshine and Shadow, it is possible to sew the hexagons in lengthwise rows, joining the rows after they are finished. A window template is extremely helpful in assuring uniform patterns and figures in the pieces.

Hexagons can also be pieced to form a diamond shape. Like the circular pattern, larger diamonds can be arranged concentrically toward the outside corners, or smaller blocks of diamonds can be joined together in an overall design. The hexagon is truly the quilter's joy because star and oval designs are also possible.

The beginner should choose either to make a quick, circular hot pad or a set of oval placemats.

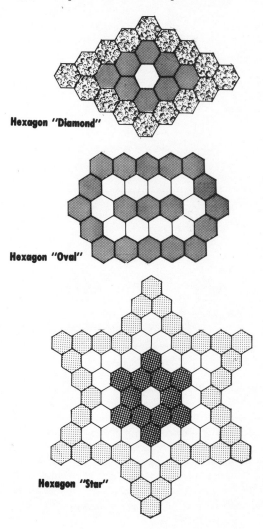

Hexagon "Diamond"

Hexagon "Oval"

Hexagon "Star"

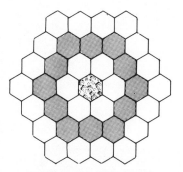

Grandmother's Flower Garden

A popular arrangement is Grandmother's Flower Garden. It consists of 3 or 4 rings of fabric. The 19- or 37-piece "flowers" are then joined with a row of white hexagons between the blocks. The blocks can be identical or randomly pieced from solid colors and printed fabrics. Quite often the center hexagon is yellow, surrounded by 2 "rows" of printed fabric of 1 color, with a fourth row of green hexagons representing the foliage. (Note: if you are making this quilt, you should not piece a complete row of white hexagons around each flower during the piecing process. You will have too many white hexagons.)

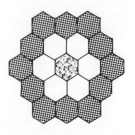

Mosaic Hot Pad

Three rows of hexagons yield an 8½″ circular hot pad. The use of a brightly striped fabric for Fabric B will create a striking effect. There is no separate quilt backing needed for this project. Your quilting will go through to the "pillow backing" and be visible on the backside. It's time to let your quilting show!

Materials
3″ x 3″ scrap of Fabric A
¹/₈ yd. Fabric B, 44/45″ wide
³/₈ yd. Fabric C, 44/45″ wide, pieces and pillow backing
12″ square quilt batting
14″ square tissue paper

Number of Pieces Required
Fabric A	1 hexagon	
Fabric B	6 hexagons	
Fabric C	12 hexagons	
Fabric C	12″ square pillow backing	

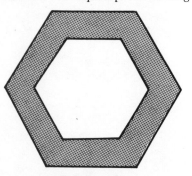

Window template

Marking the Fabric — Window Templates. The diagrams show the most efficient way to mark hexagons. Unless you are using a stripe, use the routine marking method. If your fabrics have a "directional sheen" you will be able to piece the hexagons in such a way that all of the sheen runs in the same direction. This is a built-in advantage of hexagons. Mark an "X" in the seam allowance of the north point. As you piece, you will be able to preserve the direction of the arrows.

If a stripe is used for the second row of hexagons, the pieces must be carefully marked with a window template. To make the window template, place the hexagon template on a 4″ piece of poster board. Draw around the paper template. Draw a larger hexagon approximately ¼″ outside the edges of the template. Cut on both lines. The inner hexagon will drop out of the cardboard forming the "window." Mark only the inner hexagon, i.e., the stitching line, on the fabric.

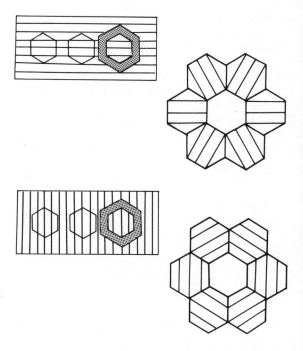

The stripes can be set in concentric rings or in lines radiating from the central hexagon. In both diagrams, the marking configuration on the left will result in the finished product on the right. In either case, extreme caution must be taken that the center of the stripe always goes through the point of the hexagon or always goes through the midpoint of a side of the hexagon. Stripes are not recommended for the third row.

Piecing. It is recommended that both the base and side of each Fabric B (second row) hexagon be pieced as it is joined to the center. That is, do not stitch all 6 hexagons of Fabric B to the central Fabric A hexagon first, going back to stitch the sides of the B hexagons together 1 seam at a time.

Piecing order for Grandmother's Flower Garden

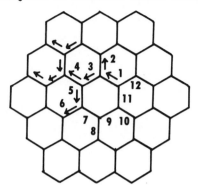

The diagram shows the right side of the "flower" with the numbers designating the order of the seams. The trick is this: Join the first B to A, then join a second B to the first B; join the second B to A, then a third B to the second B. Simplified, sew *across* the center hexagon and *out* from the center, *across* and *out*, and *across* and *out*. Once you understand this sequence, hexagons virtually piece themselves! If you are piecing stripes or fabric with a directional sheen, match each B hexagon carefully to its neighbor B hexagon before you begin to stitch.

The third row of hexagons, Fabric C, adds a new twist. Add the first C hexagon to a flat side of a B hexagon, then add a second C hexagon according to the established method. The trick lies in the next sequence. Notice that 2 sides of the second C hexagon must be joined to the B row before another C hexagon can be added. The rhythm becomes *across, across, and out* for this second C hexagon. The third is the usual *across and out*. The fourth is *across, across and out*. The distinction of the third row is that one-half of the time you are joining to a flat side of a hexagon and the other half you are joining to a "valley" made by 2 B hexagons.

Such a complicated thing. It may have been better had I simply said, "There is a tricky place where there is a tendency to add another hexagon before it is needed. Be watching!" I sincerely hope that the lengthy explanation helps you to understand why this happens. With each additional row of hexagons, an extra "valley" is inserted between the flat sides just to make things more fun. Actually, once you've made the mistake, you'll never do it again. But remember, we all do it once.

If you are left-handed, stitch according to the diagram beginning with seam #1, stitching from left to right. Then simply stitch the remaining seams in reverse order, beginning with #12 and working down to #2.

Finishing Before Quilting. Because the backside of your quilting is probably deserving of admiration by now, and because binding little hexagons is horribly tedious, you should attach the pillow backing *before* quilting. This is most easily done on the machine.

Iron the pieced top, pressing the seam allowances any way you choose. Layer the parts of the hot pad as follows:

1 Tissue paper on the bottom.
2 Quilt batting.
3 "Pillow backing" — right side up (untrimmed square).
4 Pieced top — right side down.

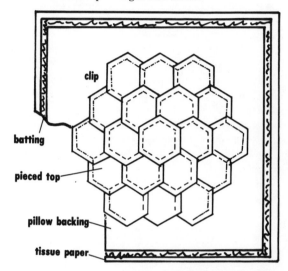

With the pieced top facing you, stitch around the points of the outer hexagons on the piecing lines, leaving an opening 2 "valleys" wide for turning. The tissue paper keeps the batting from being caught in the machine. Tear away the tissue paper. Carefully trim the batting and pillow backing to the shape of the pieced top, leaving ample seam allowances at the opening for turning. Clip the pillow backing at the "valleys" so that the hexagons will lie flat after turning. Turn the hot pad right side out. Yes, the edges will be a little ragged at first. Push out the points using a dull pencil point. Iron the hot pad. Stitch the opening closed, carefully blindstitching the front and back together.

Pin the hot pad in every hexagon and along all of the hexagon sides at the outer edge.

Quilting. The quilting of hexagons is a very intriguing thing. Only on a little "circular" pot holder should you begin quilting at the center of the flower. If you go no further with hexagons, at least read through the quilting method for the placemats to see just how ingenious quilters can be.

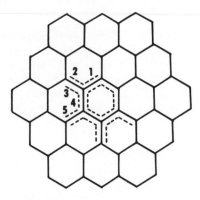

Number of Pieces Required

Fabric A	70 hexagons
Fabric B	70 hexagons
Fabric C	96 hexagons
Fabric D	70 hexagons

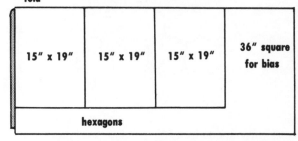

On the pot holder, begin at the center, burying the knot. Quilt around the center A hexagon, quilting ⅛″ from the seams. Slide the needle between the layers, coming out in the corner of a B hexagon. Quilt *across* and *out* on that hexagon. Slide between the layers to the edge of the adjoining hexagon. Quilt sides 3, 4 and 5 in the diagram. Continue slipping from hexagon to hexagon, quilting only the inner 3 sides of the B hexagons. When you have completed the circle, quilt completely around the outer edge of the B row, skipping from hexagon to hexagon. The Fabric B row is now completely quilted. Quilt the Fabric C row in the same manner.

Pay attention—your quilting is visible on the back. No knots, no puckers, please.

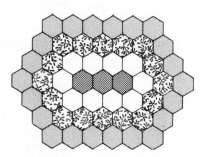

Oval Flower Garden Placemats

These directions are for a set of 6 placemats, 11″ x 15″, using 4 fabrics. The row 3 fabric is constant in all 6 placemats, with the other 3 fabrics alternating positions. No 2 placemats are identical. Because the quilting will show on the back, you may choose to use a printed or light-colored fabric for the pillow backing. Striped fabrics are not suitable for the hexagons.

Materials

⅜ yd. Fabric A, 44/45″ wide

⅜ yd. Fabric B, 44/45″ wide

½ yd. Fabric C, 44/45″ wide

2⅜ yd. Fabric D, 44/45″ wide (for pieces and pillow backing)

Cutting Diagram for Fabric D. Cut the pillow backings and square for bias before you cut the hexagons. The backings should be 15″ x 19″; the square for bias, 36″.

Multi-Template for Hexagon Cutting. Because of the larger numbers of hexagons required for the placemats, a multi-template should be cut.

On a 6″ x 10″ piece of cardboard, draw 6 hexagons, as though you were marking fabric. Allow ½″ between the markings for seam allowances. Cut out the hexagons, starting at the center of each. Use caution that the actual sides of the hexagons are smooth and accurate. Trim away excess cardboard so that all that remains is the seam allowance on the outer edges and between the hexagons.

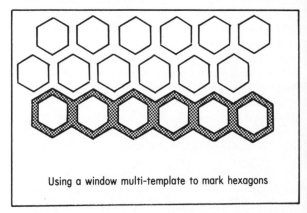

Using a window multi-template to mark hexagons

Place the template on the fabric. On the wrong side of the fabric, mark all 6 hexagons. Lift the template and lay it in position for the next set of hexagons. Because you have trimmed the excess from the cardboard, you can match up the sets of templates neatly, conserving fabric.

Of course, any number of hexagons could have been drawn on the template. Save your multi-template for your first Flower Garden Quilt.

Piecing. Follow this diagram for the sequence of fabrics in each placemat.

Placemat	1	2	3	4	5	6
Row 1	A	A	B	B	D	D
Row 2	B	D	D	A	A	B
Row 3	C	C	C	C	C	C
Row 4	D	B	A	D	B	A

Stack and thread the hexagons, one placemat to a stack, with the fourth row hexagons on the bottom. Sew the 3 center hexagons together, first, side-by-side. Add rows 2, 3 and 4 alternating the use of Fabrics A, B, and D. Fabric C will always be used in the third row.

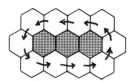

Do not piece the hexagons in straight rows. Join each row of pieces in concentric ovals. I cannot imagine a pattern which flows so easily and requires so little thought during the piecing process. True, there are a lot of hexagons, but after the concentration required by Robbing Peter to Pay Paul, hexagons should be welcome relief.

Quilting. Use a pillow backing in place of quilt backing. Pin the layers together.

Surprisingly enough, beginning at the center is not the most efficient way to quilt this design. Pin the layers together securely and begin quilting the center row at the right side. It will take 2 rows of quilting to completely quilt 1 row of hexagons. Quilt each horizontal row in the same manner, working from the center toward the bottom or top.

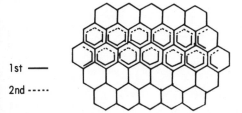

1st ——
2nd ·····

Do not quilt the outermost edges of the hexagons. These edges will be trimmed away for finishing. The cut ends of quilting threads will work loose, ruining your hard work.

Finishing. Trim the points of the hexagons off as far as the vertical seams. Trim the batting and pillow backing to the finished shape. Finish with bias binding.

1 Make sufficient bias for all 6 placemats. Cut 6 strips, each long enough to bind 1 placemat.

2 Iron the bias in half lengthwise. Fold the raw edges into the middle, so that the bias is folded in quarters. Iron.

3 Open out a piece of bias. With right sides together, place a raw edge of the bias along the trimmed edge of the quilted top. Pin the bias in place, all around the placemat. Turn under a ¼″ hem and overlap the loose ends of the bias.

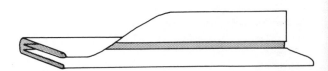

4 Using the machine, stitch along the outermost fold line on the bias. Fold the bias over the seam allowances and blindstitch in place on the back of the placemat.

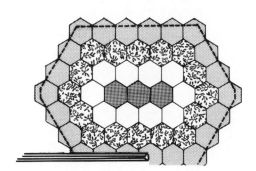

Problem-Solving. There are no usual problems.

As you browse through magazines, quilting newsletters, and books, take note of the many interesting methods that are suggested for hexagons. The usual one is the English method with all of those paper inserts and basting—ugh!

Surely you have convinced yourself that this marking and piecing technique has all the answers!

Chapter 5 / Piecing Curves

Drunkard's Path and Variations

Piecing curves is considered the most difficult form of piecework. However, if caution and logic are used, along with our marking technique, this, too, can be easily mastered.

It is recommended that the beginner make her first project from 2 fabrics. There are only 2 basic pieces involved: the "square" (#1) and the "pie" (#2). You will be cutting the same number of each piece from both fabrics; that is, 8 squares and 8 pies of Fabric A, and 8 squares and 8 pies from Fabric B. Even though this is restrictive, more than a dozen different arrangements are possible. You may select 1 of the ones illustrated or experiment on your own.

After you have mastered the simple technique, graph paper and colored pencils are all you will need to design elaborate arrangements of more than 2 fabrics or colors.

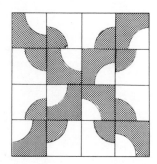

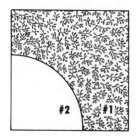

Basic unit

Note: Read the special instructions on marking before you cut any pieces.

Marking and Cutting. Notice that the paper templates in the perforated page section have arrows at the curved seamlines. These arrows indicate the center of the curve on each piece. Transferring this notation to the fabric during marking is the key to quick and easy piecing. As you trace around the template, make a small slash mark in the seam allowance perpendicular to the seamline.

Drunkard's Path Pillow

11″ Pillow (without borders)

Materials
³/₈ yd. Fabric A, 44/45″ wide; for pieces, pillow backing, and bias (optional)
¹/₈ yd. Fabric B, 44/45″ wide; for pieces
Border fabric (optional), Fabric A or B
15″ square quilt batting
15″ square quilt backing
13″ pillow backing (size without borders)

Number of Units in Block

Fabric A		Fabric B	
8 pieces #1		8 pieces #1	
8 pieces #2		8 pieces #2	

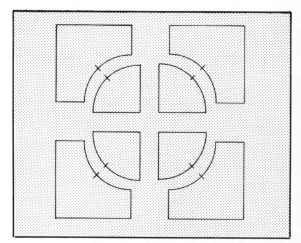

You may choose to cut a small notch in the template at the arrow. As you mark the fabric, the marker will automatically slip into the notch, with no extra effort or attention on your part. The notch must be kept small, lest the marking at the notch be too large to clearly designate the center.

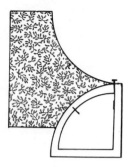

Piecing. Pin the 2 pieces together at the outer edges of the curved seamlines (right sides together). Insert the pin at the intersection (meeting point) of the curved and straight seamlines. Insert the point of the pin in the wrong side of the square (#1) *in* the seamline, about ½" down from the intersection. The pin point *must* come back up on the wrong side of the pie (#2) *in* the seamline, also ½" from the intersection. The right-hand edges are now properly aligned. Use the same technique to align the left-hand edges. The fabric will bunch up and confuse you terribly — be patient.

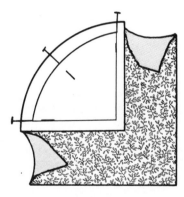

Now run a pin through the *center* markings you made during the marking process, checking the back of the square to be certain that your pin is exactly in the seamline. Add 2 more pins, always matching the seamlines. It may be easiest to add these 2 additional pins horizontally, catching very little of the fabric on the pin. If you push the head of the pin as far into the fabric as possible, you will be able to stitch exactly to the pin before you must remove it.

Stitch along the line. If you feel as though you have too many fingers and too little room, you are probably on the right track!

Piece all 16 units of squares and pies, 8 AB combinations and 8 BA combinations. Press the curved seam allowances toward the square.

Joining the Rows. After you have made all of the basic units, lay them on a table to form one of the patterns given or experiment with your own ideas. Many of the possible arrangements are actually made of 4 identical sub-blocks. Notice that Fool's Puzzle and Drunkard's Path can be divided into 4 sections of 4 basic units each. In these patterns, it is easiest to join 4 squares into sub-blocks (2 × 2), then joining the 4 sub-blocks into the main block. If your pattern does not fall into this arrangement, simply join units into 4 rows of 4 units each according to our usual method.

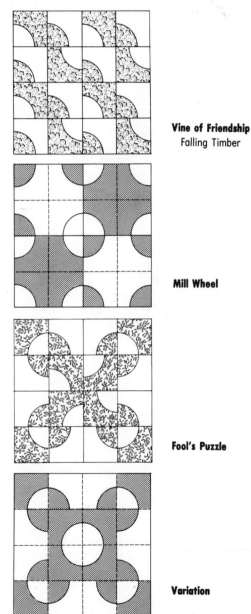

Vine of Friendship
Falling Timber

Mill Wheel

Fool's Puzzle

Variation

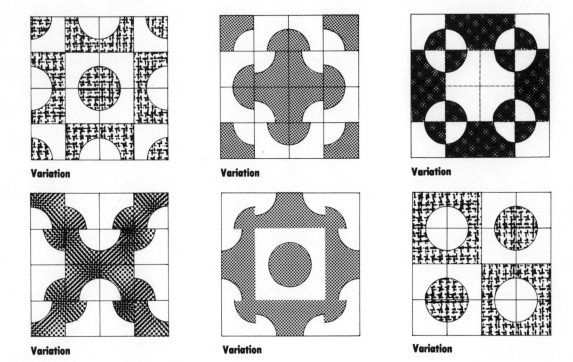

Variation Variation Variation

Variation Variation Variation

Borders. The addition of a 3″ wide border may enhance the flow of your design.

Quilting. Quilt the squares or the pies, or both, ⅛″ inside the seamlines. You may choose to create a quilting design which emphasizes the arrangement of your pieces (as in Falling Timbers).

You may find that the clamshell quilting design is especially appropriate on the borders, repeating the curves.

Finishing. Finish the block as a pillow, with the addition of ruffles or piping. Better yet, frame it! You are now a champion quilt-piecer and can attempt virtually any piecework! (If you're going crazy after 4 squares and it doesn't seem to be getting any easier, make a hot pad and call it quits.)

Problem-Solving. It is critical that the first 2 pins line up the straight sides of the square and the pie. Otherwise, the bias on the curved edges will not be eased in at the proper angle, causing distortion.

If you were to enlarge the entire basic unit for a quilt-sized template, it would be advantageous to add marks dividing the curve into quarters in addition to the middle marking. The smaller the division the less deviation will be possible.

UNIT III
Dresden Plate –
Pieced and Appliqued

Applique is the technique by which individual pieces of fabric or pieced units of fabric are applied to a background fabric. A hemming stitch (variation) or blindstitch is used to attach the fabric to the background after the raw edges have been neatly turned under. The accuracy and beauty of appliqued projects lie in the attention to detail and neatness of stitching.

Applique is a broad category which can be subdivided into at least 3 types: true applique, pieced and appliqued, and reverse applique. Dresden Plate falls into the pieced and appliqued category. It can be pieced in 16 or 20 spokes, and commonly appears in both curved and pointed spokes (outside edge). The curved outer edge is very striking, but is not suitable for a beginner's first attempt at applique. The optional center circle is usually appliqued onto the pieced plate. However, in order to broaden the range of the learning experience, and also to create a finer finished product, it is recommended that the center circle be "reverse appliqued."

This design is an extremely easy piecing project, making it an excellent beginning for the study of applique. It can be pieced in 3 different forms. The "spokes" (template #1) alone form the simplest of designs, in 1 fabric or in an assortment of 2, 4 or many fabrics. In this form, the applique background shows through the plate's center. The term *applique background* refers to the fabric on which the applique is stitched. In the second form of the Dresden Plate, #2 diamond pieces (perhaps green, as leaves between the petals) are added.

To make a third form, a yellow-centered sunflower, perhaps, a #3 circle is added to the center. In this case, it will be added by reverse applique.

Most people find that the circular pillow is more difficult to finish nicely. The effect of the circle amidst the collection of square pillows from previous lessons is a contrast that is probably worth the extra effort. One can very quickly make the pillow, or take 4 times the time to make a set of unpadded, faced, circular placemats.

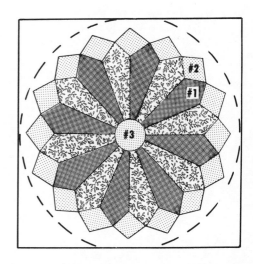

Dresden Plate Pillow

15″ Circular or square pillow (without borders)

Materials

16″ circular or square applique background, plain or printed fabric

⅛ yd. 44/45″ wide Fabric A for #1 (or an assortment of fabrics, ⅛ yd. each)

⅛ yd. 44/45″ wide Fabric B (optional)

⅛ yd. 44/45″ wide Fabric C or a 4½″ x 4½″ square of scrap material (optional)

20″ square quilt batting

20″ square quilt backing

16″ circular or square pillow backing

Polyester filling

Decorative edging

Cutting. There are 2 sets of templates for Dresden Plate. Use the small set for the 14″ pillow.

Fabric A   16 pieces   #1 (can be 1, 2, 4 or more fabrics)

Fabric B   16 pieces   #2

Fabric C   1 piece   #3

Marking and Piecing. The best way to mark the fabric for the "spokes" (#1) is to lay the template on the fabric with the point directing due north alternating with due south. If your fabric happens to be a scant ⅛ yard after preshrinking, you might try to salvage the project by lining one side of the spoke template with the lengthwise grain. The disadvantage is that you will be piecing one true bias edge with one straight edge. A better solution would be to mark the pieces in an east-west configuration.

If a printed fabric has a definite line in the print, the line should follow an imaginary radius out to the point of the spoke. It would also be possible to match stripes carefully so that concentric "circles" would be formed. Of the 2 possibilities, lines radiating toward the outer edge would add more to the total effect.

It should be noted here that if you decide to make a cardboard template from the paper one, extreme care must be taken to assure proper size. A circle consists of 360 degrees. If there are 16 equal divisions, each spoke must account for an angle of 22.5 degrees. If the long sides of the spoke are drawn even a slight distance away from the actual sides of the template, the circle of fabric will, theoretically speaking, contain more than 360 degrees. The plate, in such a case, cannot lie flat on the applique background. A slight variation from a true circle can be eased gradually over the entire appliqued surface. If you see a visible error in the size of *one* spoke, there is a good chance that the error, when compounded, will not be repairable. Fix the template.

There is no special trick to the piecing aspect of the plate. Piece the "plate" first, adding the outer diamonds in a "second trip" around the circle. Do not join the inner circle in any way until told to do so.

Preparation for Applique. You may choose to mark a stitching line ½″ around the outer edge of the applique background. If the pillow will be finished on the machine, this marking will not be necessary.

Fold the applique background into quarters. Iron the folds into the fabric.

Prepare the pieced plate for applique by ironing the seam allowance on the inner edge. To make precision points on the spokes or on the diamonds, a clever ironing trick is helpful:

1. Place the plate right-side down on the ironing board.
2. Iron all the seams between the spokes toward the left (or right, but not open). If there are diamonds, iron all of the seam allowances toward the spokes.

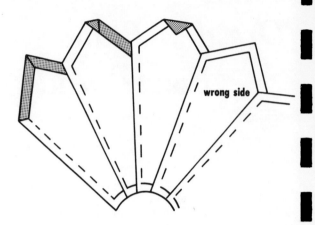

wrong side

3. Iron the very tip of the spoke (or diamond) toward the inner circle. A pin may help hold the fabric down and spare your fingertips! Spray the fabric, if your iron does that, or dampen the areas with a wet pressing cloth or a piece of muslin as you iron.
4. Iron the right edge of the spoke point (or diamond) over the ironed tip. Use the pin to hold it in place while you "steam it."
5. Iron the left side over the tip.
6. The finished effect is a mitered tip, with no nasty seam allowance at the tip to stick out.
7. Iron all the way around the plate.

Fabric of 100 percent cotton usually irons very nicely and holds the sharp creases. If the fabric does not maintain its ironed edge, quickly baste the seam allowances in place. The less basting needed in applique, the better, but if basting is needed, *do it* and be done with it.

Lay the plate on the applique background, using the ironed folds as guidelines for centering. Lay the 4 points on the fold lines, or the 4 valleys (seams between

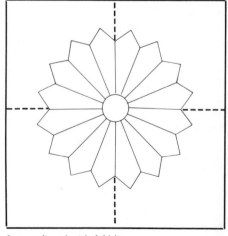

Seams aligned with fold lines

Points aligned with fold lines

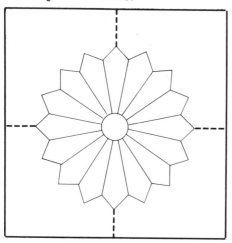

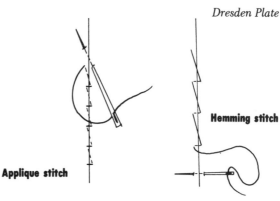

Hemming stitch

Applique stitch

spokes) on the fold lines. I have no reason to believe either is more correct or more traditional than the other. First match the north-south lines in the plate, then slide the plate up or down along that axis until the east-west fold lines are in line. Pin the plate to the applique background, with a pin in every second spoke near the points at the outer edge.

If by some misfortune the plate is just a little too big to lie flat on the applique background (template problem?), ease the excess plate fabric over the entire circle, matching the north-south axis and east-west axis to the plate pieces if possible.

Applique Stitch. Two stitches are acceptable in applique. The first, almost an overcasting variation, leaves visible stitches. To be acceptable, the stitches must be small, regular, and match the applique fabric in thread color (unless you really like the effect of careful, visible stitches in a contrasting color). The preferred stitch is the *blindstitch* which, if carefully done, leaves no visible thread on the right side of the applique. It is time-consuming but not difficult.

The "applique stitch," to give the first stitch a simple name, is actually the opposite of the simple hemming stitch used on clothing. On a skirt, for example, a small bit of fabric on the right side of the skirt and on the stitching edge of the hem is caught on the needle, with diagonals of thread showing on the stitching edge of the hem. The side you see as you sew has the most visible thread, and it is the wrong side.

In applique, the right side of the project is facing you as you sew. It is necessary to shift the long diagonal part of the stitch to the underside. Begin by knotting a single end of the thread. From the underside, which won't be visible in the finished pillow, push the needle through to the top in the applique piece, as near to the edge as possible. Insert the needle just off the edge of the applique in the applique background. Push the needle diagonally to the right to bring the point of the

needle to the topside again, about $^1/_8"$ from the previous stitch. Pull the needle through. Stitches $^1/_4"$ apart or more will not withstand wear — as the applique shifts against the applique background, the thread will weaken. Furthermore, on difficult curves and at points, the seam allowance of the applique may work itself to the outside.

If you choose to use this stitch, use thread the color of the applique, keep the stitches small, and catch as little of the applique in the stitches as possible (1/16" or less).

Blindstitch. The better choice is *blindstitching* and is not difficult. Using a knotted single strand of thread, begin by bringing the needle to the topside through the applique background exactly next to the folded edge of the applique. Pull the needle and thread completely through the fabric. Carefully take a $^1/_8"$ stitch in the applique, sliding the needle horizontally along the very edge of the fold, not actually catching the applique fabric to the applique background at all. Pull the needle and thread out of the fold (the thread is traveling inside the fold of the applique for $^1/_8"$). The second

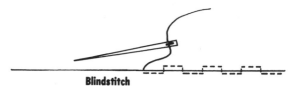

Blindstitch

stitch will be a horizontal stitch in the applique background only, directly beneath the folded edge of the applique. Pull. Make 2 or 3 stitches each in the applique and the applique background. It is not necessary to pull tightly on the thread as each stitch is being taken. After every $^1/_2"$ of stitching and absolutely before a corner is turned, tug firmly on the thread, using the thumb and fingers of the left hand to hold the applique and applique background together at the place where the stitches are being tightened. The stitches should all disappear. What you have accomplished is a "running stitch" (bottom to top, top to bottom, bottom to top) through the folded edge. Indeed, from the wrong side of the applique background, the blindstitch looks exactly like a running stitch.

To end an applique thread, simply take several back-stitches in the wrong side of the applique background beneath an appliqued piece. Use caution not to catch in the applique by mistake. Make a loop of thread and knot.

In routine applique work, the wrong side of the applique background does not show. Knots on the wrong side are completely acceptable. By all means, use the blindstitch.

Appliqueing the Dresden Plate. Begin appliqueing the plate along the outer edge of the spokes. One might usually begin at the center. For 2 reasons, you should not: first, all the pins needed to secure the outer edge of the plate are a nuisance and need to be removed as soon as possible; also, a beginner should master the blindstitch before moving on to the inner circle and reverse applique. The assumption is that you will at least *try* to blindstitch on this project.

Take stitches that are $1/8''$: that is, $1/8''$ in the applique and then $1/8''$ in the applique background. Take a stitch very close to the point of the spokes. Pull the thread to make it disappear before you turn the corners.

If no center is to be reverse-appliqued, simply blindstitch the inner circle of the plate to the applique background.

Reverse Applique. In this interesting technique, shapes are cut from the top layer of fabric to expose a layer underneath. The cut edges of the top layer are turned under and stitched in place. From a distance of a few yards, a simple design would appear the same in applique (dark units appliqued on white) and reverse applique (areas of light fabric cut away to expose dark fabric).

A very sophisticated form of this "reversing" is done in South America. *Molas* are beautiful pieces of art created by the cutting away and exposing of many layers of brightly colored fabrics in very intricate designs.

At times, particularly in working with circles, the quilter may choose to use reverse applique instead of traditional applique, to achieve a more perfect finish. In Dresden Plate, for example, it would be somewhat difficult to iron under the seam allowances on the #3 circle. Clipping would be necessary, adding the risk of ravelling.

Cut the circle from Fabric C. The seam allowance on the circle should be trimmed to $1/8''$ to $3/16''$ if the fabric will show through the spoke fabric. Simply pin the circle in place, sliding it under the curved edges of the plate. Pin the ironed inner edges of the spokes over the #3 insert. Blindstitch through all the layers, to anchor the circle securely in place. Neat trick!

Quilting the Dresden Plate. Layer the appliqued top, batting, and quilt backing, centering the top. Baste or pin-baste. Quilt $1/8''$ around the outer edge of the plate. Quilt $1/8''$ inside the inner edge if no #3 circle was added. Quilt along the outer edge of the quilt top, $1/2''$ from the edge. Additional lines of quilting on the applique background fabric may be added as the individual chooses. Some quilters quilt the spokes of the plate $1/8''$ inside the seamlines. It is individual preference which dictates how many spokes to quilt (all, or every other one); whether to quilt the entire spoke or just one side seam on each spoke; or not to quilt inside the spokes at all. A fancy design may be quilted in the center area—initials, perhaps.

Completing the Circular Pillow. If you have chosen to attempt a circular pillow, cording is the recommended finish. Avoid stitching the cording into the bias too tightly. As you baste the piping around the outer edge of the circle, the danger is in easing in too much piping or in stretching it too tightly. Little can be said in addition to this. After basting the piping in place, fold the seam allowance back to simulate the finished edge. Check for buckling and make any necessary corrections. Careful stitching of the appliqued top to the pillow back in a true circle usually brings success.

Reverse applique

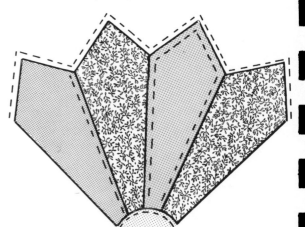

Quilt along the spoke seams or entire spoke

Problem-Solving. It is better to begin the good habit of taking tiny applique stitches now on an easy project. Stitches ¼″ in length will not be sufficient on difficult designs. If you simply *cannot* take such small stitches, stitch around the applique using ¼″ stitches, then stitch completely around the applique a second time, placing *a stitch between each pair of existing stitches.* This method has the added advantage of double strength: if a thread does break in normal wear and tear, the applique will remain "applied" due to the second round of stitching.

If your seam allowances on your applique simply will not stay ironed under, take 5 minutes to baste them in place. The whole secret of applique is in the preparation. Blindstitching itself is not difficult, but loose, uncurved curves, and unpointed points can make applique a real chore. Take the time to iron and baste—it pays off in avoided frustrations.

If the plate is puffy on the applique background after you have quilted, carefully pin the plate evenly on the applique background and add some quilting on the spokes to hold them in place.

Geometry Lesson. Lay your small spoke template (#1) on top of the large template (#1). If you slide one side of the small one along the long side of the large one, there should be a point at which the second long side will also match. The sides of the spokes, if extended inward to the center of the circle would form a 22.5-degree angle (in 16-spoke plates). Extending the sides outward would enlarge the size of the plate, but the 22.5-degree angle would remain unchanged. Remembering this simple fact will enable you to draw templates for spokes of any size.

The large spoke is also extended inward toward the center. You may trim away the inner edge of the template to any extent you like. After the plate is pieced, simply measure the diameter of the inner circle and draw yourself a new template for the #3 circle to meet your specific needs (remember to take seam allowances into account).

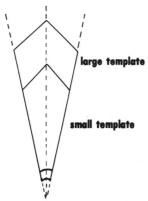

large template

small template

Therefore, as you work with the large set of templates or the small, technically the #3 circle template will fit. On the large spoke, simply trim the template at the inner edge to match the small template. Template #4 is for the small center created by the unaltered large spoke #1.

Dresden Plate Placemats
15″ Finished width
Set of 6 placemats, with
2 fabrics alternating
for the spokes

Materials
½ yd. Fabric A, 44/45″ wide
½ yd. Fabric B, 44/45″ wide
³⁄₈ yd. Fabric C, 44/45″ wide
⅛ yd. Fabric D, 44/45″ wide
1½ yd. lining fabric, either Fabric A, B, C, or D

Cutting. Use the large set of templates. Spokes must be cut from both Fabrics A and B. Each placemat will contain 8 spokes A and 8 spokes B. No quilt backing or batting will be needed.

Fabric A	48	#1 spokes
Fabric B	48	#1 spokes
Fabric C	96	#2 diamonds
Fabric D	6	#3 or #4 circles

Note: If the #3 circle is to be used with the large spoke template, the spoke template must be trimmed before the fabric is marked.

Procedure. Piece all 16 of the spokes and diamonds on all 6 placemats. The center circles will be reverse-appliqued after the linings are joined to the tops. Cut 18″ squares of lining. Place a placemat and a lining square together, right sides together. Pin the pointed outer edges to the lining. Using the machine, stitch around the points. DO NOT STITCH THE INNER EDGE. Trim the points and clip the valleys. Turn the plate right side out. Iron, pushing the points of the spokes out with a dull pencil point. Lay the #3 or #4 circle in the center. Reverse-applique the circle in place, stitching through all of the layers.

Quilted Placemats — Options. If you prefer quilted placemats in this pattern, you could layer and stitch them in the manner of the hexagon pot holder. Use the center for turning and reverse-applique the center circle before quilting. It would also be possible to layer each placemat in the traditional fashion, using pillow backing fabric instead of quilt backing for a professional finish; however, binding the edge nicely would require tremendous skill and patience.

UNIT IV Lap-Quilting
Chapter 1 / Dresden Plate Quilt

Lap-quilting is the method recommended for apartment-dwellers and others who do not have the space available for a traditional frame. Its other advantage is that the project remains portable through the quilting stage. An item as large as 24″ square could be quilted as one piece. For anything larger, the project should be divided into basic units which are joined after the quilting is completed.

The success of the lap-quilting technique lies in the quilter's ability to recognize a basic unit and to repeat her joining technique with uniformity. Unfortunately, lap-quilting requires a sizable excess of both batting and backing: every unit needs 4″ to 5″ of excess at the quilting stage, all of which is trimmed away. Also, considerable time is spent in the block-joining process.

If the extra time and added expense do not outweigh the advantages of lap-quilting, the technique is one well worth learning.

The technique is suggested for virtually any quilt-sized project which can be divided into square or rectangular units. The back of the quilt will be marred by the joining seams, but if these seams are carefully blindstitched and "lined up," the total effect is not at all unbearable.

Description. Dresden Plate is a wonderful pattern for a beginner's first quilt. The "plate" is pieced quickly and can be beautifully done in scrapbag style. Appliqueing the plates is not difficult. The overall effect of the circle is very pleasing, making Dresden Plate a well-loved pattern of long standing.

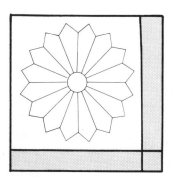

Basic Unit

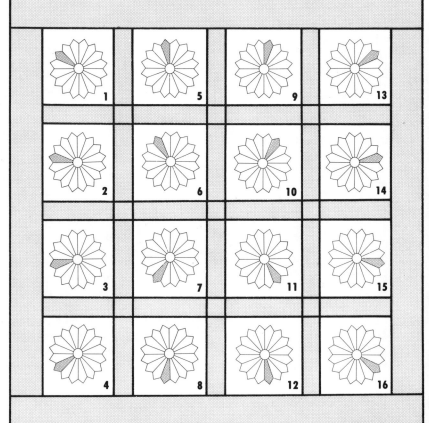

Before the quilter can purchase her fabric, she must carefully analyze the quilt's design. Borders, lattice strips and squares, and the number of blocks are all variable elements. Study of the basic technique should enable the beginner to change any of these elements to suit her individual needs.

Study the diagram of the basic unit. In this case, the basic unit consists of the appliqued block, a vertical lattice strip, a horizontal lattice strip, and a lattice square. Nine of these units exist unaltered in the quilt. Six more units consist of an appliqued square with one lattice strip, either vertical *or* horizontal. One unit consists of only the appliqued block. The quilter must always be aware of which of the units she is making.

The borders are added in place of lattice strips and lattice squares on the outer edges, and they are treated as separate units. Because it is difficult to miter corners in lap-quilting, this quilt was designed with simple straight borders.

Lap-quilting does not require lattice strips *or* borders. Nor do the strips and borders have to be simple pieces of plain fabric. A pieced or appliqued lattice or border should be sewn as an independent unit. It should then be joined to the quilt top proper as a single unit. Nor does the main unit in the quilt top have to be an appliqued block. Any of the square blocks in the beginning chapters could be used in a lap-quilt.

The finished size of this quilt should approximate 88" square. This figure allows 5 percent shrinkage due to quilting. It should fit a full-sized bed with a dust ruffle. It will require separate pillow shams. Instructions for other sizes can be found at the end of this chapter.

General Fabric Requirements

Fabric for Spokes: approximately 2 yards total of 2, 4, or more fabrics, according to your design. The total number of fabrics must be divisible by 2.

Fabric for Applique Background: $3\frac{7}{8}$ yards, 44/45" wide

Fabric for Borders and Lattice: $4\frac{7}{8}$ yards, 44/45" wide

Quilt Batting: one piece 81" x 96" and one piece 90" x 108", either cotton or polyester

Quilt Backing: 6 yards, 90", wide after preshrinking

Cutting and Marking the Fabric

Fabric for Spokes. The full-sized quilt uses the small spoke template. A total of 256 spokes will be needed for the quilt (16 spokes for each of the 16 blocks equal 256 total). Whether the spokes will be 16 different fabrics in random arrangement or a very few fabrics in carefully controlled sequence will determine how much fabric is required. If all 16 spokes are to differ, 16 fabrics, each $\frac{1}{8}$ yard will be needed for a total of 2 yards. The total would be less if fewer than 16 spoke fabrics were to be used, due to less waste.

If the spokes are to be cut from an assortment of fabrics, it is advised that the lattice/border fabric be used as spoke fabric as well. This is simply for the sake of continuity.

The fabrics for the spokes should be viewed on the applique background as they are selected. For an even more thorough preview, lay the applique background fabric on the border fabric to examine the total effect. A spoke fabric must not blend into the applique background lest it "disappear" in the plate and give the appearance of a missing tooth. Consideration must be given to balancing hues, shades, brightness and prints versus solids.

If the center circle and the ring of diamonds around the plate are part of your design, you will need to determine how much fabric you will need to purchase (see page 95).

Mark and cut the spokes according to the usual method. Arrange the spokes into "plates" and stack and thread them.

Applique Background. The applique background can be either a light or dark fabric. It may be solid or printed. You will be able to create a variety of effects by varying your fabric combination. To test the overall impact of your fabric, cut one spoke from each of the spoke fabrics and arrange them on your applique background. If any one spoke matches the background too closely in color or scale, it should be eliminated. A nice balance should exist between the plates and the applique background. Even if the applique background is a dark printed fabric, the plate can and should be the focal point.

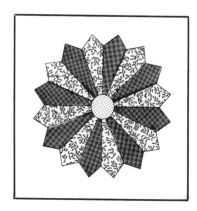

You will need a clear marking on the wrong side of the applique background to indicate a piecing line. On the right side, you will need to see a quilting line around the outer edge of the block. The fact that the quilting will be completed before the blocks are completely surrounded by lattice could result in uneven spacing between the quilting and piecing lines. To simplify marking and to assure uniformity, a dual marking template should be cut. The edges of the applique background will be clipped to indicate both the piecing and quilting lines. These clips are visible on both sides of the fabric. The clips, of course, must be very small.

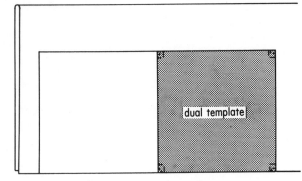

To make this "dual template," cut a perfect 16″ square from a sheet of poster board or heavy brown wrapping paper. Mark the sides of the template with small pencil lines exactly ½″ and 1″ from all 4 corners (for a total of 8 sets of markings). The marks ½″ from the corners designate the piecing line. The marks 1″ from the corners designate the quilting lines.

Fold the preshrunk and ironed applique background fabric in half lengthwise, wrong side out. Two applique background squares will be cut at one time. Draw around the 16″ template 8 times. *The line is the cutting line*, so adjoining squares will share a side. Cut the fabric.

If your fabric has a "directional sheen," or is a directional print, you should mark the "north" or topside of all of the blocks in the seam allowance on the wrong side of the fabric with a small arrow. This arrow will indicate the orientation of the block in the finished quilt.

If you have cut carefully, and if you have good sharp scissors, you will be able to clip the blocks 4 or 8 at a time. Lay the template on the pile of blocks. Clip the fabric square at all 16 markings, about ¼″. *Care must be taken not to clip beyond the piecing line* (which hasn't yet been marked).

Begin the applique background marking procedure by placing the fabric right side down. These first lines can be drawn in pencil or other unwashable marker. Using the 18″ ruler, draw a line connecting the clips ½″ in from the edge. Draw the line all the way to the edge of the fabric. Turn the fabric and mark the other 3 sides. These lines are the piecing lines. If the seam allowances are a little uneven, do not despair. The square formed by the lines should be exactly 15″. *That is the important thing.* This method is used because it

allows quick "mass production" cutting and permits the correction of irregularities in cutting at the marking stage.

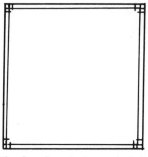

wrong side of applique background piecing lines

right side of applique background quilting lines

Turn the fabric over so that it is right side up. Connect the *inner* set of clips with a washable marker. If you have been unable to obtain a washable marker, use the pencil very lightly, remembering that the lines will be indelible. Do not draw the lines to the edge of the fabric — stop at the intersection of the lines. These are the quilting lines. The reason we have clipped the edges to mark them is that the clipped markings are readable on both sides of the fabric. If you will hold the fabric up to the light, you will see that the inner square is precisely centered in the outer square. Hooray!

Cut out the quilting template #1 from the perforated page section. Place this paper template in one corner of the applique background, with the quilting lines facing you. Line up the 2 straight sides of the template against the horizontal and vertical quilting lines in the corner. Draw the toothed-edge and inner curve of the template on the applique background. Mark the other 3 corners.

Carefully fold the applique background into fourths, matching the clips rather than the corners (remember — we aren't trusting the accuracy of the cut edge). Iron creases into the applique background to simplify the centering of the plate on the backing in future steps. Lay the applique background aside. Do the same to prepare the other 15 applique background squares.

Borders and Latticework

Templates for Lattice. The templates for the latticework will follow our general rules. You will mark the piecing line and not the cutting line. Cut the two following templates from poster board:

- 5″ square — lattice square
- 5″ x 15″ — lattice strips

Marking and Cutting the Border — Latticework Fabric.

- 2 11″ x 76″ strips — side borders
- 2 11″ x 99″ strips— top and bottom borders
- 24 lattice strips
- 9 lattice squares

The most expedient way to cut the border fabric is to fold the lattice/border fabric in half lengthwise (selvages together), and then again lengthwise into fourths. Cut off a strip 99″ long, that is, the length of the longest border. Then cut along the fold lines, using great caution not to shift the layers of fabric, to yield 4 strips. Each strip should be 99″ long and approximately 11″ wide. The exact width is not critical, so long as all 4 are equal. Cut 2 of the strips to a total length of 76″. The leftover pieces of fabric can be used for latticework and spokes.

Mark lattice strips, lattice squares, and spokes on the fabric using the cutting diagram as a guideline, being certain that you allow for seams. Cut the pieces by the usual cutting method, cutting *between the lines.*

Marking Quilting Design on Lattice Strips, Squares. Fold a lattice strip in half vertically and in half horizontally to divide the strip into fourths. Iron or finger-crease the folds to facilitate marking of the quilting lines. Using template #2 from the perforated page section, mark the quilting design on the lattice strips. On the lattice squares, mark quilting lines 2¼″ inside the cut edge (to make a 1½″ square) and 1″ inside the cut edge (to make a 4″ square). Note the peculiar sizes of these squares, and be watching for an explanation at the joining stage.

Batting and Backing. Because each quilt unit will be quilted individually, a generous excess of both batting and backing must be allowed for each block. In order that ample quilt backing be available to turn under even seam allowances at the joining stage, a 5″ excess per unit is recommended. As you become more advanced, you may choose to lessen this amount to eliminate waste.

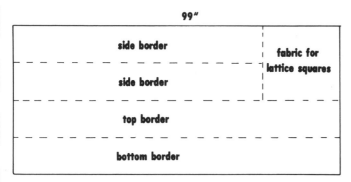

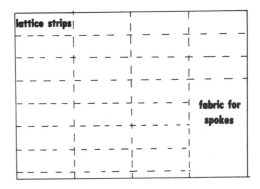

Cutting Guide for Border and Lattice Fabric (allows ½″ for seams)

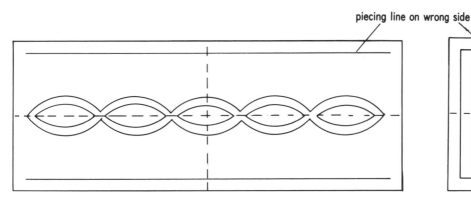

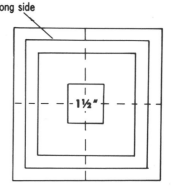

Quilting Lines on Lattice Strip and Squares

Cut the following units from both the batting and backing:

Unit	Number to Cut	Cut Size
Basic unit (blocks 1, 2, 3, 5, 6, 7, 9, 10, 11)	9	26″ × 26″
Single lattice strip (blocks 4, 8, 12, 13, 14, 15)	6	20″ × 26″
No lattice strips (block 16)	1	20″ × 20″

Cutting Guide for Batting

Cutting Guide for Quilt Backing

Appliqueing the Block. Follow the directions in the Dresden Plate Chapter to piece and applique the block. Notice that the "plate" can be centered on the applique background with the spoke points on the fold lines or with the seams between the spokes on the fold lines. On your own project, you may do either. If you have selected a random sampling of fabrics with the inclusion of border fabric for one spoke, you will want to regulate the position of that spoke in each block. My feeling is that there is no such thing as random placement. The mind works patterns into things, even though subtly. So that the spokes made from the border fabric are evenly dispersed across the quilt top, spokes have been shaded in the quilt diagram to indicate the position of the border spoke in each block. This may seem a picky detail, but planning will prevent an unhappy coincidence later on.

Adding the Latticework. Notice that the quilt diagrams include a picture of the basic unit. Blocks 1, 2, 3, 5, 6, 7, 9, 10, 11 will be constructed exactly like the diagram. Blocks 13, 14, 15 will have the horizontal lattice strip but no vertical lattice strip or lattice square. Blocks 4, 8, and 12 have only a vertical lattice strip. Block 16 is quilted with no latticework at all.

With the wrong side of the applique background facing you, pin one lattice strip to the side of the applique background, right sides together. Stitch on the pencil line, all the way to the edges of the fabric. Sew the lattice square to the second lattice strip. Matching the seams precisely, sew the second strip (plus square) to the applique background and lattice unit.

lattice

Quilting the Basic Unit. It is vital that the appliqued and pieced unit be centered on the quilt batting and backing. There must be a generous 2″ excess on all 4 sides. Generously pin the layers together.

It is important that you be aware that the wrong side of this quilting project will show in the finished product. *All knots must be buried.* Care must be taken that the quilt backing remains smooth. Three basic areas must be quilted:

1 The applique block: Quilt ⅛″ inside the circle made by the spokes. Quilt ⅛″ around the outside of the spokes. Quilt the marked square around the block, and all of the lines made by quilting template #1. Quilting *on* the plate itself is optional.
2 Lattice strips: quilt the design on the lattice. Divide the design into 4 parts: quilt the upper half of the inner ellipses, skipping between the layers from one to the next; then complete the lower half of the ellipses. Finish by quilting the outer lines.

3 Lattice square: Quilt only the inner square. The outer square will be quilted after the blocks have been joined.
4 Do not quilt the outer square on the lattice square now. Wait.

Quilt all 16 of the units according to the components of each. Continually strive to improve your quilting stitch. The tendency is to move too quickly along the straight lines on the applique background where the going is easy. After a block or 2, measure your stitches in 3 or 4 different places. The average beginner reaches a level of 6 stitches per inch on this project. This level seems to remain standard unless a truly conscientious effort is made to improve. It should be repeated that a "stitch" refers to one stitch on the top plus the gap between that stitch and the next one. Give yourself ample credit as well, if the stitches are all even and regular, and if the quilt backing is smooth with even, visible stitches.

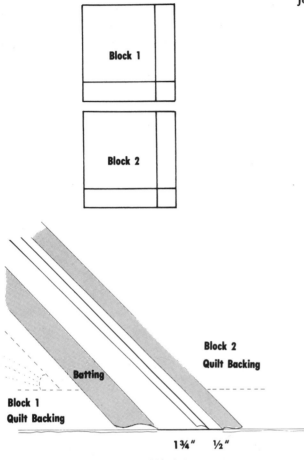

Joining top layers of block 1 and block 2

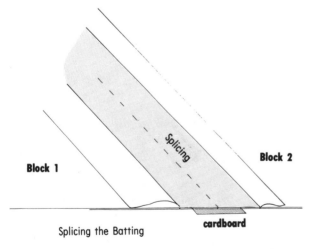

Splicing the Batting

Joining the Blocks.

1 Begin with blocks #1 and #2. Lay the 2 blocks on the table as they should appear in the finished quilt. Holding the top edge of #1, invert it onto #2, right sides together, so that the free edge of the lattice strip on #1 is on top of the upper edge of block #2.

2 Sew the applique background of #2 to the lattice strip of #1, being careful not to sew in the battings and quilt backings of either piece. (This could be done on the machine if care is taken to pin the units carefully on the seamline.) Sew all the way to the edges of the fabrics.

3 Lay the partially joined blocks on the table right side down in such a way that the top of the quilt points to the left. The bottom of the quilt is on the right. Pull the quilt batting and backing of each block away from the seam. Finger-press the seam allowances toward the lattice. (Note: if the lattice were light and the applique background dark, the allowances could just as easily be pressed toward the applique background.)

4 Lay a strip of cardboard 2″ wide and the length of the lattice on top of the joined quilt tops. This cardboard serves to protect the quilt top from scissor points. Overlap the batting pieces, trimming one slightly if there is too much excess to permit smooth overlapping. Sliding one blade of the scissors along the cardboard protector, cut through both layers of batting at the same time, from one end to the other. Remove the trimmed edges. Butt the cut edges of the batting together. This cutting is called splicing. If you have not cut perfectly straight, the battings should still match up: the zig on one will match the zag on the other. Remove the cardboard.

5 Stitch the battings together with a ½″ long whipstitch. Be careful that you bring the batt edges together, but do not create a raised seam. Stitch bottom to top, and then top to bottom for extra strength. Take care not to stitch beyond the end of the piecing line on the quilt top. As you later trim the excess batting, you would automatically cut off the knots, allowing the seam to work loose.

6 Smooth the quilt backing away from the seam area with your hand. It should naturally form a fold at the quilted square of the applique block (on the right), and along the bottom

curves of the quilted loops of the lattice strip (on the left). Laying the cardboard strip under this folded backing, mark a line 1½″ from the quilting on each side. It is imperative that the backing be folded back in a straight line lest too little seam allowance be left for even joining. Trim the excess quilt backing from both the right-hand and left-hand blocks.

7 Lay the right-hand seam allowance back over the batting. Fold under ½″ on the left-hand allowance, then lay it over the right-hand allowance. The two should overlap by ½″. Alter the amount of turn under on the left-hand side if they do not. The regularity with which you can produce this trimmed and folded seam will determine how nice the backing of your lap-quilted coverlet will be.

8 Blindstitch the seam, beginning at the seamline of the blocks, stitching to the other seamline. Do not stitch the backing beyond the seamlines. Because some of the backing will be trimmed as rows are joined, threads would be cut, allowing seams to creep open.

9 Join the 4 blocks of row #1, consistently joining with the top of the quilt to the left as you trim and overlap the seams in the backing.

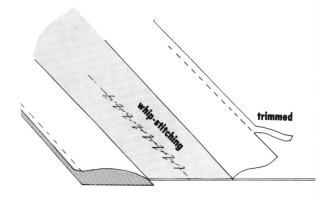

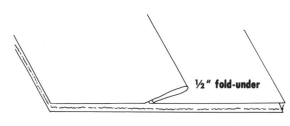

Overlapping the Quilt Backings

Joining Rows. The same basic steps should be followed to join rows together. Join rows #1 and #2, then #3 and #4, and then #2 and #3. This order will keep the bulk of the quilt off your lap for the longest possible time.

Consistency must be maintained to keep the seams in the backing regular. For example, if rows #1 and #2 are being prepared for seaming in the backing, the bottom of the quilt should be near your body, the top of the quilt extending away from you. Right side down, row #1 would be on the right and row #2 would be on the left. As the left seam allowance is pinned over the right, it should be possible to line up the backing seams between the blocks. As you blindstitch, secure any gaps that were not stitched as blocks were joined and any loose seams where threads were accidently clipped.

At this time you should quilt the second square of quilting lines on the lattice square. When you folded back the quilt backing along the quilted lines in order to mark and trim off the excess, it was important that the fold line was uniform all along the lattice. Had the second quilting design (outer square) already been quilted, it would have been difficult to mark the cutting line with absolute uniformity. This "going back"

should be considered an important aspect of the lap-quilting technique. If there had been no lattice square at all, the loop design might have been extended, uninterrupted, along either the horizontal or vertical lattice strips. In such cases, the quilting lines should be drawn at the usual time, but the quilting should be interrupted several inches from any block joinings. After joining, the needle can be rethreaded and the quilting extended across the seam. In fact, this extension of the quilting over the seamlines after joining does help to minimize the piecework appearance of the quilt back.

Cutting Side Borders. Lay the border fabric (76″ long) on a double sheet of batting, lining up the long edges very carefully, allowing 1″ to 2″ in extra length on the ends. Cut the double layer of batting 1″ larger than the border on the 2 short ends, but the same size on the 2 long sides. Use the same method to cut the backing, eliminating careful measuring of fractions of inches when precision isn't that necessary. Cut strips of tissue paper 1″ wide and as long as possible, cutting enough total length to reach completely around the outside of the quilt (350″ to 400″).

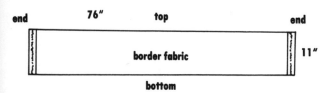

top
end   76"   end
border fabric   11"
bottom

Marking Piecing and Quilting Lines. Fold the border fabric in half, crosswise and lengthwise to mark the middle in each direction. Although two borders will actually run north and south on the quilt, and two will run east and west, for the purposes of teaching we will consider all of the borders to be the same until the time comes when they are actually joined to the quilt. The "top" of the border will be the long side which will be joined to the quilt. The "bottom" edge is the edge which will ultimately become the outer edge of the quilt. The short sides of the borders will be called the "ends," and one will be the "right end" and the other the "left end." Therefore, we can say that the long fold divides the border horizontally while the short fold divides the border vertically. Making these distinctions will make the rest of the explanation much more simple.

Using the horizontal fold line as a guide, draw quilting design #2 on the border. Start at the center, working toward the right and then to the left. Extend the design by placing the first loop of each repeat over the last loop of the previous set. It should be noted that as you draw the fourth loop each time, you should *not draw* the center point. The outer pair of curves should make a continuous line, only meeting at the very beginning and end of the pattern. Likewise, the curve at the very center should not come to a point. Draw the loop design to within a few inches of the ends of the borders. *The design will need to be extended after the top and bottom borders have been joined.* You will be able to do a smoother job of matching up the quilting designs if you wait until the final stages to draw on the designs.

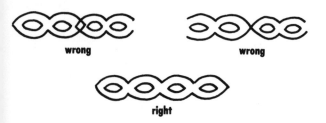

wrong   wrong

right

Mark a quilting line on the right side of the border on the topside, 1½" from the cut edge. The quilting line will actually lie 1" inside the stitching line on the finished quilt. This line of quilting will secure the batting in preparation for the joining of the border to the quilt blocks.

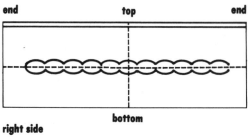

end   top   end

bottom
right side

On the wrong side of the top of the border, draw a seamline ½" from the cut edge. Using the vertical fold to indicate the middle of the border, draw slash marks on the seamline to indicate the points at which the applique blocks and lattice strips should be matched.

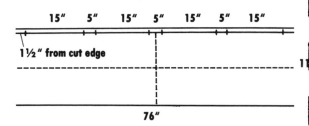

15"   5"   15"   5"   15"   5"   15"

1½" from cut edge

76"

That is, beginning at the center and moving toward the right, mark 2½", 15", 5", and 15". There should be a slight bit of excess length beyond the last 15" slash. Make similar markings from the center to the left, beginning with 2½". These markings will enable you to piece the border onto the quilt evenly.

Layering, Stitching the Border. Lay the border fabric right side up on a table or on the floor with the piecing line at the top. Lay the quilt backing (right side down) and the quilt batting exactly along the long side at the bottom. Pin every 4" to 6" along the bottom edge. Using the machine, stitch the 3 layers together in a ½" seam, sliding strips of tissue paper between the batting and the presser foot. Stitch completely from one end of the border to the other. The tissue paper prevents the presser foot from tearing the batting. Tear away the tissue paper.

Turn the border fabric up over the batting, bringing the right side of the border to the top. Roll the border fabric slightly toward the backing underneath, creating a ½" hem of border fabric on the underside. Pin this rolled edge to keep it from slipping. Smooth the border fabric against the batting. If you choose, place several pins along the top edge of the border. The batting and backing should extend 1" beyond the edge of the border (due to the rolled edge).

You may have noticed that the quilted loop design is no longer at the lengthwise middle of the border. The rolling has shifted the middle slightly. The marking method you have used is still the best, because it compensated for individual variation in the actual width of your borders and anyone else's. Remember that the width of the border is simply ¼ the total width of your border fabric after preshrinking. We never actually measured that width. Therefore, to try to estimate in inches the exact distance the loop design should have been drawn from the cut edge would have been futile. The small inaccuracy of the placement of the middle quilting design is unimportant.

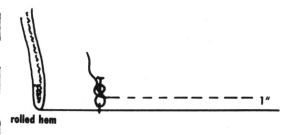

Quilt a line 1" from the rolled edge to hold it permanently in place. Begin and end this quilting line a few inches from the right and left ends of the border. End by simply pulling the thread out of the needle, leaving a "tail" of thread to be used to finish quilting the line after the top and bottom borders have been joined. *Do not quilt completely to the ends of the border* — leave 4" to 6" unquilted at each end.

Begin quilting the loop design 4" to 6" from the actual end of your market design. The reason you must stop 4" to 6" from the edge is that you will try to bring the quilted loop designs on the top and bottom borders to a point in the corners of the quilt. This may require some adjustment in the length of a loop or two, either by squeezing or stretching. The finished effect will be smoother if the adjustment is spread over an area of a few inches.

Quilt the inner and outer curves of the design, remembering that even if you mistakenly drew points on the outer curves at the end of each repeat of the design, you *must not* quilt them. Leave a tail of thread when you have quilted to within 4" to 6" of the end. After the top and bottom borders have been added, these tails of thread can be rethreaded on a needle and used to continue the quilting line. This decreases knotting (and possible puckering) and eliminates an obvious break in the flow of the quilting design.

Quilt the line 1½" from the cut edge of the top of the border, beginning and ending 4" to 6" from the ends.

Joining Side Border to Quilt. Following the routine piecing method, join the border fabric of the side border to the quilt top (top layers only). End your piecing exactly at the beginning and end of the quilt top (at the piecing line on the applique blocks at both ends). Any excess border fabric on the ends will be trimmed in following steps.

Splice and whip the edges of batting together, stopping at the exact beginning and end of the quilt top. Fold the seam allowances of the quilt backing against the quilting lines on each side.

To determine how much backing is needed to properly make a seam, measure the distance between the quilting line boundaries on the right and left of the joining area. Add ½" to half of that distance. That total is the seam allowance needed on each of the right- and left-hand pieces of quilt backing. In this case, the total distance between the quilting line boundaries is 1½". Half of that distance is ¾". Adding ½" to half the distance gives us ¾" + ½" = 1¼" total on each side. This will permit a ½" turn-under and a ½" overlapping.

Mark a line 1¼" from the quilted line on each seam allowance and trim away the excess backing. Lay the backing from the quilt top over the batting. Fold ½" under on the border backing and lay it in place. Blindstitch only from the actual beginning to the actual end of the quilt top.

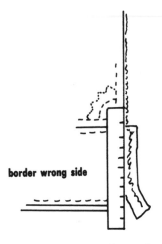

border wrong side

Using a ruler or T-square or your best judgment, trim any excess from the ends of the borders so that the line of the bottom of the quilt extends in a straight line to the outer edge of the border. If you have been very careful in the stitching processes, no threads joining the top fabrics, battings, or backings will be cut. If one should be, or if there is a gap in the stitching, thread a needle and do some "doctoring." Repeat the entire procedure for the other side border.

Top and Bottom Borders. Follow the directions on side borders to prepare the top and bottom borders for joining to the quilt:

1 Fold the border in quarters and crease it to facilitate marking.
2 Mark the piecing line, adding pencil slash marks to designate the matching points for the border and quilt top.
3 Draw the chain of loops along the horizontal fold line, this time stopping 9″ from the ends of the borders.
4 Mark the quilting line 1½″ from the top edge.
5 Stitch the 3 layers together, completely, from end to end.
6 Roll and quilt the bottom edge, beginning and ending the quilting 9″ from the outer edge.
7 Quilt the loop design, ending 9″ from the edge.
8 Quilt the line 1½″ from the top edge, *between the slash marks indicating the quilt top only,* leaving a tail of thread.

Joining Top and Bottom Borders. Pin the top border in place, using the pencil marks to match the border to the blocks and lattice strips. Pin only through the quilt top and the border fabric. Carefully pin the top border to the trimmed edge of the side border, being careful not to stretch either one. Pin the top border exactly at the fold

of the rolled edge. There should be a minimum of 2″ excess at both ends.

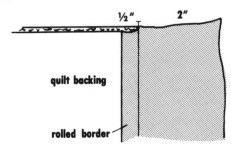

quilt backing

rolled border

Piece the top border onto the quilt, beginning and ending exactly at the fold of the rolled edge.

Lay an 18″ ruler alongside the edge of the top border on one side, lining up the long edge of the ruler with the exact outer edge of the side border. Draw an extension of the side border onto the quilt backing of the top border to indicate the cutting line for trimming.

Cutting only the backing and batting, trim the excess at the end of the border. When the scissors reach the rolled edge of the top border, carefully snip away the batting from the seam allowance without cutting away any border fabric.

do not clip folded hem

quilt backing and batting
trimmed even with side border

trim excess
border fabric
to 1″

Trim the extension of the border fabric to 1″. The border fabric which is rolled under at the outer edge should be rolled under the same amount on the extension. Fold a mitered corner, turning under ½″ of the border fabric on the extension. Fold the extension over toward the backing at the very edge of the batting to complete the rolled hem at the end of the top border. Blindstitch all the loose edges of the border fabric, stitching the miter as well.

Finish quilting the borders, using the "tails" of quilting thread whenever possible.

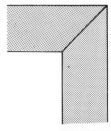

front

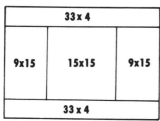

Pillow Shams

Piecing. Complete the Dresden Plate as usual. Applique to the background fabric. Join the 2 side borders and the top and bottom borders before quilting. Gather and baste the ruffle in place or apply decorative edging to the quilted top.

Prepare the backing sections. On the 24″ side of one piece, turn under a double ¼″ hem. Do the same on a second piece. Overlapping the 2 backings about 2″ at the center back, pin the pillow backing in place. Stitch.

An additional 12″ to 18″ in length is required if the quilt is to tuck under the pillows. An entire row of blocks would have to be added, only to be hidden beneath the pillows. Pillow shams are a nice alternative.

Brief instructions are given for a pair of shams which will fit standard-sized, 20″ x 30″ pillows.

Materials

½ yd. applique background
4½ yds. border/lattice fabric

or

2½ yds. border/lattice fabric and 6½ yds. decorative edging
32 spokes from appropriate fabrics
¾ yd. quilt backing batting

Cutting. The actual cut size of the strips of ruffled fabric is 7″ x 44″. For all other pieces, add ½″ seam allowances as you mark the fabric.

Piece	No. to Cut	Dimensions Width x Length
Applique background	2	16″ x 16″
Side borders	4	10″ x 16″
Top and bottom borders	4	5″ x 34″
Backing pieces	4	19″ x 24″
Ruffle strips (actual size)	10	7″ x 44″

Machine-Piecing. Although many beginners are eager to take timesaving shortcuts by piecing on the machine, very few are still willing to sacrifice the accuracy at this stage of the game. It should be said, however, that there are many very proficient quilters who do much of their piecing with the machine.

Particularly if you are a competent seamstress, the joining of borders (top of quilt only) to a quilt top is easy to do on the machine. In fact, you may choose to join the top layers together beginning with the very first two blocks.

The warning is this: Pin the units as you would units to be hand-pieced, matching corners and lining up seamlines. Use a generous amount of pinning. The tremendous bulk and weight of the quilt top puts a strain on the machine, and it is difficult to stitch even, straight lines. Furthermore, you will have to struggle to keep the batting and backing layers out of the stitching line.

You alone shall be the judge regarding machine-piecing. Many have decided that after so much attention to detail, the time would be better spent joining the blocks and borders completely by hand.

back

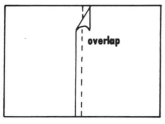

overlap

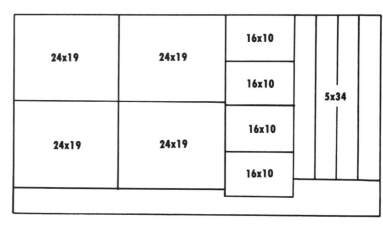

Cutting Guide for Border Fabric
(2 Pillow Shams)

Varying the Size of Dresden Plate Quilt. If you choose to make a twin-sized or king-sized quilt, use the information in the table below in determining how much fabric to buy.

Dresden Plate Quilt Coverlets

Mattress size	Twin (Small templates) 39" x 75"		Full (Small templates) 54" x 75"		King (Large templates) 76" x 80"	
	Width of Quilt	Length of Quilt	Width of Quilt	Length of Quilt	Width of Quilt	Length of Quilt
Size Finished Appl. Block	15"	15"	15"	15"	18"	18"
No. of blocks per row	x 3	x 4	x 4	x 4	x 4	x 4
Total Inches for Blocks	45"	60"	60"	60"	72"	72"
Width Lattice	5"	5"	5"	5"	5"	5"
No. Lattice Strips in Row	x 2	x 3	x 3	x 3	x 3	x 3
	10"	15"	15"	15"	15"	15"
Width of Borders (9" each)	18"	18"	18"	18"	18"	18"
Finished Dimensions	73" x 93"		93" x 93"		105" x 105"	

If you desire a quilt which tucks under the pillows, eliminating the need for pillow shams, add a row of blocks to the length of the quilt.

Twin Size. (Use the small set of templates.)

Spokes: Up to 2 yds. total of 2, 4, or 16 fabrics; cut 192 spokes

Applique background: 3 yds. fabric, 44/45" wide

Border/lattice fabric: 3½ yds. fabric, 44/45" wide

17 lattice strips	5" x 15" finished size
6 lattice squares	5" x 5" finished size
2 borders (top and bottom)	9" x 79" finished size
2 borders (sides)	9" x 77" finished size

Batting-backing:

Basic unit: appliqued blocks, 2 lattice strips and a lattice square	6	26" x 26"
Single lattice strip	5	20" x 26"
No lattice strips	1	20" x 20"

King Size. (Use the large-sized templates.)

Spokes: Up to 4 yds. total of 2, 4, or 16 fabrics; cut 256 spokes

Applique background: 4¾ yds. fabric, 44/45" wide

Border/lattice fabric: 5½" yds. fabric, 44/45" wide

24 lattice strips	5" x 18" finished size
9 lattice squares	5" x 5" finished size
2 borders (top and bottom)	9" x 111" finished size
2 borders (sides)	9" x 89" finished size

Batting-backing:
(Note: the batting for the top and bottom borders will have to be pieced.)

Basic unit: appliqued block, 2 lattice strips and a lattice square	9	29" x 29"
Single lattice strip	6	23" x 29"
No lattice strips	1	23" x 23"

Completed Projects

Pella Tulip pillow appliqued and quilted by Joy Kidney.

(Front (l. to r.): Sunshine and Shadow pillow by Janis Waldorf; Tooth Fairy pillow by Kirsten Hassel; Sunshine and Shadow pillow by Janis Waldorf. *Center:* Simple Star pillow by Janis Waldorf. *Back (l. to r.):* Simple Star pillow by Pam Dyer; Simple Star pillow, Kathleen Pease.

Left: Cathedral Window pattern, eyelet-edged pillow by Marilyn Lee. *Right:* Another approach to Cathedral Window pattern by Joy Kidney.

Clockwise: Hexagon pot holder, Carla Hassel; Puff-Patch pot holder, Carla Hassel; Hexagon pot holder, Susan Ackelson; Nine-Patch pot holder, Carla Hassel.

Front (l. to r.): Drunkard's Path pillow by Janis Waldorf; variation of Drunkard's Path pattern by Marilyn Lee. *Back (l. to r.):* Fool's Puzzle pillow by Carla Hassel; variation of Drunkard's Path pattern by Pam Dyer.

Center: Hexagon pillow by Marlene Luczek Foley is ringed by Hexagon placemats by Janis Waldorf.

Robbing Peter to Pay Paul pattern is shown in a variety of interpretations. *Front (l. to r.):* Pillow, Marsha Jambretz; wall hanging, Katherine Smithen Verser; pillow, Carla Hassel. *Center:* Pillow, Susan Ackelson; pillow, Carla Hassel. *Back:* Two pillows by Joy Kidney.

Christmas and harvest Puff-Patch wreaths made by Carla Hassel.

Front (l. to r.): Round Dresden Plate pillows by Joy Kidney, Janis Waldorf; placemat by Carla Hassel. *Back (l. to r.):* Square Dresden Plate pillow by Marlene Luczek Foley and pillow with plate pieced by Kirsten Hassel, at age five.

Dresden Plate Friendship Quilt was created by Doreen Stokes, Sheryl Simpson, Nancy Mitchell, Marsha Jambretz, Marlene Luczek Foley, Susan Ackelson, Elisabeth Spoerl, Katherine Verser, Marcia Collins, Kathleen Pease, Parlee Kennedy, and Carla Hassel. Owner: Parlee Kennedy.

UNIT IV

Chapter 2/Dresden Plate Friendship Quilt

The lap-quilted Dresden Plate Quilt is easily adapted to a group-effort quilt. Whether it is a wedding gift, golden anniversary remembrance, or even a baby gift, a quilt made by a group of dear friends and relatives would please anyone.

One person should be responsible for purchasing and preparing the fabric. That person should also cut the latticework and applique background. It would also help to assure uniformity if she also transfers the outer quilting and piecing lines to the applique background. The individual quilters should be able to finish marking the quilting designs on the applique blocks and the lattice.

An interesting scrapbag quilt can be made "potluck" style. Each participant should bring 2 or 3 sets of cut-out spokes, 16 spokes in each fabric. This will be too many if there are actually 16 quilters; this allows some spokes to be eliminated if they are not appropriate for the applique background.

As the blocks are completed, each quilter would take a turn joining blocks and rows together. The borders could be joined at a quilting bee for a traditional touch.

A neighborhood group or women's group could easily cooperate to make a quilt. Tickets could be sold to determine a recipient, or a merit system could be used. For each block made or joined, the quilter would earn a credit. Upon the completion of the quilt, the names would be put in a hat, one chance for one credit, and a lucky winner would be picked.

You should find that if a group of quilters all follow these methods of marking and piecing, the workmanship should be uniform enough to permit the exchange of piecework and applique. At least one "guild" exists in which quilters combine their efforts to make quilts for each other. One such is the Great Iowa Quilt Factory, in Des Moines, Iowa. One person designs her quilt and cuts out the pieces. The blocks are then distributed to a dozen willing workers who piece or applique the blocks. The group meets a month or two later to join the completed blocks. The quilt is then quilted by the owner or by the entire group at quilting bees in the owner's home. Each member earns a quilt (of her own design and at her own expense) by completing 16 blocks or basic units for her friends' quilts. The more energetic the individual, the sooner she will earn her quilt. There are marvelous advantages to this organization: Each quilter is constantly challenged by new patterns; she is exposed to designs and colors she might never have chosen on her own; and she never tires of a quilt because her work is finished after a block or two! If you are fortunate enough to have a half dozen friends who are willing to try such a cooperative, the Dresden Plate quilt would be an ideal beginning. Upon its completion, the group would be able to discuss the feasibility of continuing on a more elaborate scale.

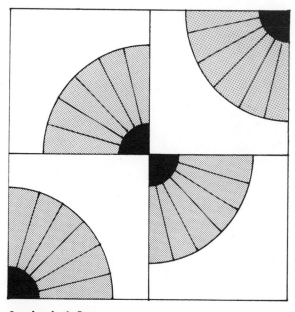

Grandmother's Fan

UNIT V
True Applique

Pella Tulip. This Pennsylvania-Dutch style pattern is an original design named after Iowa's Dutch community, Pella, founded in 1847 near Des Moines. It is purely applique, combining a variety of problems and challenges: curves, points, overlapping pieces, non-reversible pieces, and bias. The key to success lies in the preparation techniques.

There is no specific quilting pattern given in the book. The beginner should plan and quilt her own design.

Pella Tulip Pillow

16″ – 19″ Pillow (optional border)

Materials

$^1/_8$ yd. Fabric A (#1), 44/45″ wide

$^1/_4$ yd. Fabric B (#2 and borders)

$^1/_4$ yd. Fabric C (#3)

17 – 20″ cut size pillow backing (buy extra of A, B, or C)

17″ cut size square applique background (white, beige, or other light color)

20 – 24″ square quilt batting

20 – 24″ square quilt backing

Single fold bias tape for stems; green or color of your choice

Polyester filling

Marking and Cutting. If you desire stems in a fabric which is not available in bias tape, you may cut stems of your own. In this case, it is not really imperative that the stems be cut on the bias—they do not need to bend or curve in this design. Simply cut straight strips from the template in the perforated section. Iron under $^1/_4$″ seam allowances on the long edges.

Fabric A	Leaf (#1)	4 pieces
Fabric B	Sepal (#2)	4 pieces
Fabric C	Tulip (#3)	4 pieces
Bias tape	2	7″ long pieces

Procedure. In order to become familiar with several different techniques for applique preparation, you should cut and prepare each part of the design individually. After you have experimented with each method, you will be able to state a preference more intelligently and combine techniques confidently as you continue your quilting career.

Preparing Applique Background. It is not necessary to mark a piecing line around the outer edge of the applique background if you plan to complete the pillow by machine.

Locate the tracing pattern for the applique background in the permanent template section (p. 112).

Fold the applique background in quarters both horizontally-vertically and diagonally. Iron in the folds. Place the tracing diagram beneath one quarter of the applique background so that the dotted lines are concealed by the diagonal fold lines. Trace the design onto

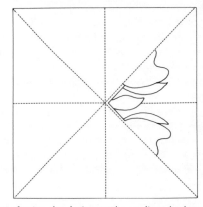

Transferring the design to the applique background

the right side of the applique background with a washable marker. If you have not purchased a washable marker, draw only the basic landmarks in very light pencil. Mark the leaf tip, the three points of the tulip, sepal points, and the bottom edge of the tulip. Because pencil will never wash out, its use must be kept to a minimum.

Move the pattern to another quarter and trace the design. Repeat until the design is completely transferred to the applique background.

Preparing Leaves for Applique. Notice that the leaf is not symmetrical. It has a definite left and right side. If you fail to flip the template to its long side as you mark your fabric, your applique will be the mirror-image of the original design. Cut the template from the page, marking it "Right side—Flip template" and "Wrong side—This side up" on the appropriate side. Any time you create an original applique design, you must be aware of this potential problem.

Paper-Pressing

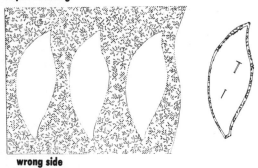

wrong side

From coarse, brown, grocery-bag paper, cut 4 leaf templates (#1). Mark each template to indicate right and wrong sides. Mark on the wrong side of the fabric, and cut 4 leaves from Fabric A, leaving ¼″ seam allowances between the leaves. Turn the iron on to a cotton setting. Dampen the leaf fabric pieces thoroughly. If you have used a water soluble pen, it will not matter that the marking disappears. Place one piece, right side down, on the ironing board. Lay the brown bag template on the fabric, right side down, centering it in the seam allowances. Place one pin in the center. With the tip of the iron, press the seam allowances over the edge of the template, ironing the tip as you did the points on the Dresden Plate spokes. After all of the edges have been ironed, remove the pin and place the iron firmly on the leaf to dry it out. How neatly formed your leaves are depends a great deal upon the delicacy with which you push against the edge of the template. Roll the tip of the iron in a wavy motion. Don't ram the sides of the piece or the leaf will be withery indeed. Complete the preparation of the other 3 leaves in the same manner.

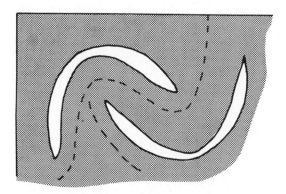

Preparing Sepals for Applique. Following the basic method used to prepare the leaves, cut 4 sepals (the green, cup-shaped leaf under the blossom) from brown paper. Pin the templates to Fabric B in 2 or 3 places on each. Do not draw around the template. Simply cut around the template, leaving seam allowances. Dampen the fabric and iron. Remove the pins and firmly press the body of the piece, drying it. If you are using 100 percent cotton, the ironed edges should be crisp. The paper will stay tucked inside the fabric until you choose to remove it. If your fabric is not cooperating, remove the paper template and neatly baste the seam allowances in place. Brown paper is recommended instead of index cardboard simply because it is dried so easily by the hot iron and because several can be accurately cut all at one time. If cardboard were used, each template would need to be individually cut. Furthermore, the cardboard doesn't dry readily.

Preparing Tulips for Applique. The tulips are symmetrical and, therefore, reversible without creating problems. To conquer the curves, a second method of applique preparation is recommended.

Cut the template from the book. *Do not cut brown paper templates.*

On the right side of the fabric, draw 4 tulips, allowing for seams. Cut around the tulips, leaving no more than ¼″ allowance. Following the diagram, clip the curves, never clipping within 1/16″ of the marked template line.

You are going to finger-roll the seam allowances to the wrong side of the tulips. Begin on one of the relatively straight portions of the tulip. With the thumb and forefinger of your left hand, roll the seam allowance to the back, pinching tightly to hold it securely when the drawn line and the fold exactly coincide. Baste a stitch or two as far along the edge as is properly folded, about ¼″ in from the folded edge.

Work the rolling just ahead of the basting needle. At a very sharp curve, take very small basting stitches, as close to the fold as necessary. Return to a distance of ¼″ from the edge on the straight stretches. Baste completely around the tulip. Dampen the fabric and iron it dry.

The finer job you do of rolling and basting, the more perfect your curves will be. On a concave curve (as the valleys between tulip points), it is careful clipping that will allow the curve to be gentle and even. It may help to "stretch" the fabric over the left index finger, pulling with both thumbs to put tension on the fabric as you baste. If a clip has overstepped the marked boundary you must finger-roll it to the underside, even if that means rolling beyond the marked line. If the slash is too deep, discard the piece and start again. An exposed clip on an appliqued piece represents the beginning of the end.

Preparing the Stems. If you are using ready-made bias tape, simply cut 2 lengths, 7″ each. Avoid any seams in the bias.

If you are cutting your own stems, use the template from the book to cut 2 strips of brown paper bag. Prepare the stem fabric in the manner of the leaves and sepals, cutting on either the straight grain or the bias, whichever you choose.

Appliqueing Pieces to Applique Background. Always study the diagram to determine the order in which the pieces must be applied. In Pella Tulip the following order is essential:

1 Leaves: All four leaves must be applied first.
2 Sepals: Each sepal must be carefully centered on the stem line and appliqued before the stems are laid in place.
3 Stems: The stems overlap the leaves and sepals, extending slightly into the tulip area.
4 Tulips: Center the tulips carefully along the diagonal fold lines, slightly overlapping the edges of the sepals.

Appliqueing the Leaves. The most expedient procedure is to applique all of any given piece at the same time in the order described. Remove the paper template from the first leaf and pin it in place. Match the point of the leaf to the point of the tracing on the applique background. If the leaf tilts to the left, shout "Hooray!" You did everything properly. If not, don't start over. In this design, the tilt of the leaf tip is of little consequence. However, in many patterns there would be no mercy—the fabric would be ruined.

The stem end of the leaf should extend well into the stem crossing in the center of the design. It is not necessary to stitch this end under—it will not show. In fact, it is better *not* to stitch it under due to the increased bulkiness of all of the layers. Simply open out the seam allowance, baste over the end, and continue appliqueing. It would have been possible to cut and turn the leaf so that the stem end fitted snugly into the right angle at the stem crossing, with no fabric extending beneath the stem at all. This is not recommended for two reasons: It is too difficult to predict accurately, and the slightest gap interrupts the flow of the design.

Appliqueing Sepals and Stems. Remember that the seam allowance of the sepal beneath the tulip applique does not need to be carefully blindstitched. It may be opened flat (to reduce bulk) and quickly basted (to save time).

Fold the stems in half lengthwise to locate the center. Lay them in place, covering the ends of the leaves and overlapping the sepals. Pin them in place.

On bias tape, special attention must be paid to the applique process. Because bias "gives" as you sew, the fabric is automatically stretching in the direction in which you are sewing. After one side of the bias has been appliqued, you must begin blindstitching at the same end as the first. If you do not, one side of the bias will be stretching one way while the second stretches the other. The result will be puckering.

Why would we choose to use bias tape? On gentle curves, the bias gives just enough to actually lie flat on the applique background. On a very tight curve, even bias will not cooperate. Then it would be easiest to prepare a template and cut the exact shape needed.

Of course, if you have prepared straight-grain stems, you may applique up one side of the stem and down the other.

It is important that the stem overlap the sepal. Fold the end of the stem under at the sepal to discover how different the design looks if the stem "dead-ends." The line of this design should flow from tulip to tulip.

Positioning the Tulips. How you position your tulips on the sepal will individualize your pillow. Some people ignore the tracing diagram, placing the tulip snugly on the sepal, practically eliminating the sepal at the tulip base altogether.

Others set the tulip high on the stem, exposing much of the sepal fabric. Experiment until you discover your own preference. Do not follow the tracing design so closely that a gap is left between the tulip and the sepal.

Any deviation in ironing or rolling can cause minor inconsistencies in the sizes of the applique. Correct the placement of any pieces by overlapping pieces slightly wherever they touch.

Applique the tulip in place, stitching through the sepal to the applique background to secure all the layers firmly in place. If your blindstitches are more than $1/8$″ apart stitch a second time around, placing a stitch between two existing stitches. An embroidery hoop may be used, but it is not necessary.

Other Applique Preparation Techniques. There are two other preparation techniques which are more commonly recommended. "Paper-pressing" and "finger-rolling" seem easier and more exacting, but for the sake of thoroughness, you should be aware of stay-stitching and basting-in-place.

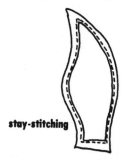

stay-stitching

basting-in-place

Stay-stitching lightly outside the stitching line prevents raveling after clipping. This is usually done on the machine, and does not in itself assure sharp points *or* smooth curves. To avoid having the little point of fabric poke down into the machine by the needle, draw the design and stay-stitch around the line before you cut the fabric into the individual pieces. I feel this is time spent which does not really enhance the quality of the finished product. You will still have to press or otherwise shape the pieces prior to applique. If you clip carefully, and if your stitches are close together, the applique piece will stay in position securely and will not fray.

The "old way" was to baste the applique piece in place on the applique background without turning under any seam allowances. The basting must be more than a seam allowance distance away from the planned finished edge (it's already tricky to guarantee proper placement). Using the point of the needle to draw the raw edges under, fold under and blindstitch the edge all in one step. I feel this method does not guarantee good points or curves for a beginner or for a pro.

Preparing for Quilting. Add borders if you plan to do so. Center and stack the layers. This project is very large and probably requires actual basting rather than pin-basting.

Quilting the Pella Tulip. In applique, it is customary to quilt $1/8$″ to $1/4$″ around the appliqued pieces and never to quilt on the pieces themselves. (There are always exceptions—in this case, the Dresden Plate and others.) Additional quilting lines can be added at $1/4$″ to $1/2$″ intervals which imitate the original quilting line. These lines create a rippling of fabric as the lines flow toward the outer edges.

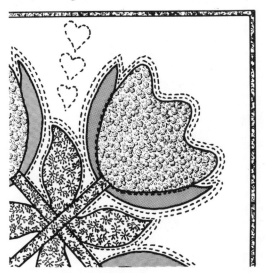

To create this rippling effect, quilt around the major pieces, even stitching into the tight corners between the stems and the leaves. Quilt between the sepal and tulip along the base of the tulip to define the applique more clearly. Due to the large size of the tulip piece, it is recommended that some quilting be done on the tulip to prevent shifting. A heart, mini-tulip, and petal lines are all good choices. After the applique portion is quilted, quilt a line 1″ from the cut edge of the applique background. Add quilting lines, working from the inside out, adding quilting lines every $1/2$″. If an appliqued piece interrupts a line of quilting, slip the needle under the piece as if no interruption had occurred. Use your own judgment as you near the edges, perhaps quilting a wavy square between the flowers and a wiggly triangle between the flower top and the corner of the applique background.

You may choose instead to quilt windmills or wooden shoes in the spaces between the tulips. Bouquets of tulips fit nicely into the very corners of the square. Use your own imagination to create whatever quilting design you choose.

When you have finished, examine the wrong side of the pillow top. Imagine it as a block in a quilt. The quilting line between the tulip and sepal clarifies the design on the quilt back. There should be no knots or puckers. This is probably your last official quilting as a beginning student. Check yourself on the following points:

1 Are all of the knots concealed? (Good!)
2 Are the stitches small enough to satisfy you? (Good!)
3 Are the quilting lines evenly spaced? (Good!)
4 Is the quilted top all bunchy at the edges? (Bad!)
5 Did the quilted top lie down nice and flat before the pillow backing was joined? (Good!)
6 Are you proud of your work? (Hooray!)

Finish the Pillow. You may wish to use remnants of Fabric B for bias piping, or add a ruffle or decorative edging of your choice.

The Challenges of Pella Tulip. Pella Tulip covered a lot of territory. It is assumed that you will have a definite preference for either paper-pressing or finger-rolling, but your exposure to both has made you a more competent quilter. As you design your own patterns, or as you make templates for designs you have seen elsewhere, carefully extend all pattern pieces so that the appliques overlap. Special attention must be paid to asymmetrical pattern pieces.

The non-circular design of the Pella Tulip pattern permitted slight irregularity in applique size and placement. Had the design been circular, placement would have had to have been exact. Even the slightest overlapping, when compounded several times around the circle, would have ruined the design.

It is not always necessary to trace the entire applique design onto the applique background. For Pella Tulip, fold lines — horizontal, vertical, and diagonal — might have been sufficient. The horizontal-vertical lines would have indicated leaf placement. A simple measurement along the diagonals would have indicated sepal placement. Diagonal lines would also indicate stem placement. The midpoint of the tulip would lie along the diagonal.

The overlapping of light fabrics on dark fabrics sometimes causes a problem. Trim away as much of the dark fabric as possible.

By the time you have finished Pella Tulip, you have struggled with many of the frustrations of applique. If you can remember that the simple key to success lies in the preparation of the appliques for stitching, applique

can be a real joy. With practice, you will soon be capable of smooth curves and pointed points, smooth bias, and accurate placement. If you do enjoy applique, you have the added benefit of easier quilting: there are no seam allowances through which to quilt.

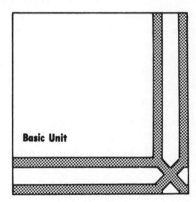

Basic Unit

Pella Tulip Quilt

The Pella Tulip Quilt with its Garden Maze lattice-work is an example of the simple techniques of lap-quilting used to create something quite intricate. (See Front Cover.) A very brief description is given so that you will be encouraged to stretch your imagination. A detailed pattern will not be given.

The applique background in the quilt is 18″ square instead of 17″ to permit a wider variety of quilting designs. The quilt is subdivided into 16 units, the basic unit consisting of the applique background, a vertical lattice strip, lattice square, and horizontal lattice strip. The lattice strip is simply 3 separate strips joined to form a rectangle. It is the lattice square that creates the difficulties.

The lattice square consists of one long, double-pointed "spear" and two short, single-pointed "spears." Four white "lattice triangles" complete the square. Two of these lattice triangles complete the design of the adjoining lattice strips. The other two lattice triangles actually belong to the lattice strips of adjoining blocks.

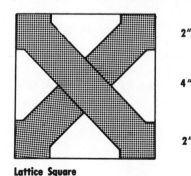

2″

4″

2″

Lattice Square

Blocks on the left and upper edges of the quilt all have 3 or 4 lattice strips instead of 2. The total size of the upper left-hand block with its 4 lattice strips and 4 lattice squares is approximately 32″ (a bit large for lap-quilting).

Great pains were taken to match the seamlines on the quilt backing in the quilt photographed. The beauty of the backing was further enhanced by the elaborate quilting on each of the blocks. It was necessary to end the quilting on the lattice strips 2″ from the joining edges to facilitate joining. The lattice triangles belonging to adjoining blocks could not be quilted until the joinings were completed. The subsequent quilting had to penetrate the extra layers of seam allowances. Although this was somewhat difficult to do, the carry-over of the quilting from one block to the next definitely minimized the scarring of the quilt backing by the seams.

The finished quilt is 110″ x 110″. It contains 42 fabrics. The colors of the tulips are arranged in diagonal rows; this gives the quilt a pleasing color balance. The deep green lattice fabric had a "directional sheen" which required special marking and cutting to avoid a hodgepodge finish. In the corners, the outer half of the lattice square was trimmed away before binding for an unusual finished edge.

The quilt was made by 15 people as an example of lap-quilting at its finest. I extend my deepest thanks to the people in 5 states who gave so willingly and unselfishly of their time and talent. They are truly "Super Quilters."

UNIT VI
Puff-Patch

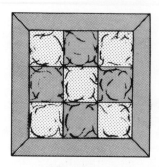

Puff-Patch Hot Pad
Christmas or Harvest Wreath
Puff-Patch Pillow
Coverlets

Puff-patch does not involve quilting at all, but is a piecework type of thing, so it is included in this manual. Old puff quilts were often made of satins and velvets and other "unquiltable" fabrics. The warmth came from bunches of batting stuffed into the individual puffs. No large sheet of batting was used beneath the quilt top as such. Puff-patch (or biscuit quilting) is becoming popular today for perhaps two reasons: It requires no quilting, and it can be done quickly and easily on the sewing machine. While some quilters frown upon the rather thrown-together appearance of such coverlets, I feel that puffs can be treated as squares in a nine-patch, and intricate piecing designs can be arranged.

The basic theory behind the puff is that a large square cannot be sewn evenly to a smaller square. In order to make the edges meet, pleats must be made in the sides of the large top square. These pleats create an excess of fabric in the center of the top square, forming a space to be stuffed or puffed.

The beginner can make a hot pad in an hour by hand — it's a quick project which will familiarize the beginner with the traditional hand method. The wreath should be done on the machine (of course, it *can* be done by hand), because it involves so many puffs. Suggestions for a pillow top or coverlet are discussed so that the puff enthusiast can strike out on her own more confidently.

Puff-Patch Hot Pad

Certainly by now you have sufficient scraps from other projects to piece this little hot pad. Any scrap bigger than 3″ square is sufficient to cut a puff top. Any scrap bigger than 2¼″ square will be fine for the puff backing, and it need not be quilt backing as such.

Materials
Fabrics for puffs and puff backing (scraps)
7½″ square of pillow backing
2 7″ squares of batting for extra thickness (optional)
Polyester filling for puffs

Templates. Cut 2 cardboard templates, 3″ (puff top) and 2¼″ (puff backing) squares. In this lesson, the outside edge is the cutting line, and not the sewing line. It is important to remember this fact when you mark your fabric for cutting.

Cutting
Puff top fabrics — 9 3″ squares (actual size)
Puff backings — 9 2¼″ squares (actual size)

Procedure. To make the puffs, place a top fabric square against a backing fabric square, wrong sides together. Pin the squares together at the corners, angling the pins toward the center. On 3 sides of the square, fold the excess top fabric into a pleat and pin it to the backing. It doesn't matter which way you make the pleats, simply aim for the center of the side. Using a long running stitch, sew along 3 sides of the square, making as narrow a seam as possible (¹⁄₈″ is ideal). Stuff the puff lightly with polyester filling. Pleat the fourth side and stitch the puff closed. Make all 9 puffs.

 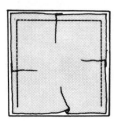 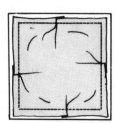

Making puffs — hand method

Assembling the puffs into rows follows the traditional method of piecing squares. Arrange the puffs in 3 rows of 3 puffs each. Pick up 2 puffs which need to be sewn together. With the puffs' right sides together, sew ¼″ from the raw edges along one side, just inside the running stitches holding the puff tops and puff backings together. Lay the puffs flat on the table, right side up. You now have concealed the raw edges at that seam. Continue to sew the puffs into rows and then sew the rows together. The puffier the puffs, the more difficult it will be to sew the rows of puffs together. It should be possible to match the corners of the puffs as the rows are joined to each other, as in traditional piecing.

Trim the layers of quilt batting to the size of the completed puff-patch top. Place the pillow backing on the table right side down. Center the layers of batting and the puff-patch top on the pillow backing, right side up. Fold the excess pillow backing over the outer edges of the puff-patch top, turning under a narrow edge. Miter the corners if you wish, and blindstitch the pillow backing in place.

Although the puff-patch will be too bulky for removing hot pans from the oven, it is ideal for protecting the table or countertop from warm casseroles. If the puff fabrics are arranged into designs, the miniature puff quilt is a very attractive novelty.

Puff-Patch Christmas Wreath

This wreath is a practical application of the puff technique. In the Christmas wreath, the red puffs are spaced prettily across the front of the wreath to simulate holly berries amidst the greenery. The puffs are sewn to make a long "snake," with the colors of the puffs carefully ordered. The snake of puffs is then wound around a styrofoam wreath and secured. The backs of the puffs will not be visible, so virtually any scraps of fabrics can be used. The puffs will never actually be joined in rows, so extreme accuracy is not necessary in the pleating process, and the squares need not be exactly uniform in size. If this mass piecing technique really intrigues you, it would be a quick and easy way to make an entire coverlet of puffs.

Materials

¼ yd. each of 7 green fabrics, prints or solids, 44/45″ wide (for puffs)

½ yd. red fabric, print, or solid, 44/45″ wide (for puffs and coordinating bow)

1 yd. puff backing fabric, either quilt backing or scraps from the puff tops

Polyester filling

16″ tubular styrofoam wreath (16″ diameter to the outside edges of the tube)

Large dressmaking pins (plastic heads or plain)

White glue

Plastic ring (about ½″, for hanging wreath)

Templates. Cut 2 cardboard squares, 3¾″ and 4½″. The outer edge is the cutting line, *contrary to our usual method.*

Cutting the Fabrics. Cut the fabric for the bow. Read the section on bias bows on page 80 to determine how much fabric to cut. Cut this fabric first and set it aside.

Arranging Fabrics for Mass-Cutting. Notice that in the diagram the red fabric puffs (designated by ▨▨▨▨) form a circle on the front of the wreath, alternating with green puffs. You may choose to have the puffs between the red puffs all of one green fabric, or of all 7 of the green fabrics in an alternating sequence.

The fabrics will be grouped into 10 basic units consisting of 8 puffs per unit. A red puff will begin each unit. The fifth puff will automatically fall next to the red puff as it is wound around the styrofoam wreath. That is to say, it takes 4 puffs of fabric to wind once all the way around the tube. If you have a favorite among the greens, designate it as fabric #5 and create your chain of puffs so that red is always #1 and your chosen green is always #5. If you choose to alternate the green fabrics so that the puffs between the red puffs on the front of the wreath vary in fabric, you will change the sequence of the greens after the mass-cutting process.

Pile the 8 fabrics on top of each other, right sides up, with the red fabric on top. If you have decided that you like a regular sequence of green fabrics, place the chosen green as the #5 fabric in the pile (red is #1). Place the cardboard template on the top fabric and draw around it. Draw another square next to the first, leaving no space between the squares for seam allowance. Draw a total of 10 squares on the red fabric.

It must be continually emphasized the lines which will be drawn are the cutting lines. Because the puffs are well suited for machine piecing, no stitching lines will be marked. It is important, therefore, that the edges be accurate. With your very best sharp scissors, cut through all 8 fabrics, being careful to keep the layers in line with one another. If you are not varying the sequence of the green fabrics, simply stack the 10 piles of fabric together, 80 puffs in all.

If you *do* want to vary the sequence of green fabrics, lay the 10 piles of fabrics in a row on the table. Take the red square off each pile and lay it alongside its pile. To vary the sequence of the green fabrics, do the following:

Leave pile #1 alone, and place its red square back on the top of the pile. Turn the entire pile upside-down on the table.

Pile #2: Remove the first green square and place it on the bottom of the pile. Replace the red square on the top of the pile, turn the pile over and lay it right side down on pile #1.

Pile #3: Remove the first and second green squares and place them on the bottom of the pile. Replace the red square, turn the pile over, and lay it on the second pile, right side down on the table.

Continue shifting the green in the piles until a group of 6 greens has been put under square #7.

Piles #8, #9, #10: The logical sequence of the alteration would leave the next pile untouched, with the cycle completed. However, because we are ultimately forming a circle, these next 3 piles will fall very close to the first 3 piles. Therefore, shift 2 greens to the bottom of pile #8, 3 greens to the bottom of pile #9 and shift 4 greens to the bottom of #10. They will lie across the wreath from their duplicates.

Cutting the Puff Backing. Cut 80 3¾" squares from the puff backing fabric. You may fold the fabric into fourths or eighths to facilitate mass cutting. Draw around the template, leaving no seam allowance, and cut on the lines.

Sewing the Puffs — Machine Mass-Piecing. The beginner should familiarize herself with the traditional method of puff-piecing before she attempts this quick-and-easy, mass-production method.

Mass-Piecing the Puffs.

1 Lay the pile of puff tops to the right of your sewing machine. Lay the pile of puff backings next to the first pile.

2 Thread the machine with regular thread. If you are very particular, the bobbin thread should match the puff backing fabric instead of the top fabrics. Remember that this is really of little consequence — the backs of the puffs will not show on the wreath.

3 Pick up the first red square and place it right side up on the first backing square. Match the upper right-hand corner as you did in the hand-piecing method. Lay the square in front of the presser foot, allowing a ⅛" seam allowance on the right side.

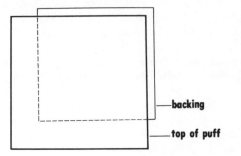

—backing

—top of puff

4 Lower the presser foot. Sewing a ⅛" seam, sew about ½" along the first side. With the presser foot down, fold the pleat and, using your finger to hold the pleat in place, sew over it. Continue sewing to ⅛" from the lower corner.

5 Lower the needle into the fabric. Lift the presser foot and pivot the fabric so that you will be able to stitch the next side. Lower the presser foot.

6 Make the next pleat and stitch the second side. Pivot, pleat, and sew the third side in the same manner. Sew completely to the edge of the third side. Do not raise the presser foot. Do not remove the completed square. Do not clip the threads.

7 Align the top and backing of the next puff and slide its upper right-hand corner under the front edge of the presser foot. Ideally there will be a gap of ⅛" to ¼" between the two

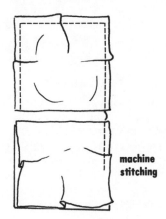

machine stitching

puffs. Begin sewing the next puff. The presser foot will pull the puff under the needle. Pleat and stitch 3 sides of the second puff.

8 Continue making the puffs until all 80 are pleated and stitched. The string of puffs will remind you of sheets on a clothesline. You have saved time and thread by stitching the puffs together in this manner and have eliminated the least-fulfilling aspect of this project — thread cutting! An extra advantage is that you have preserved the order of the fabrics, and you are ready for the next step.

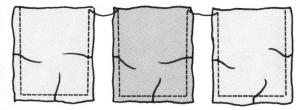

Joining the Puffs.

1 Pick up the first red square. With the unsewn fourth side pointing north, lay the right side of the red square on the right side of the adjoining green square. Side #3 of the red square will coincide with side #1 of the green square. The $1/8''$ length of thread between the squares gives you the leeway you need to lay the puffs flat together. Sew the seam from top to bottom, backstitching at the beginning and end, in a $1/4''$ seam. On the right side, the initial seams will not show.

opening for stuffing

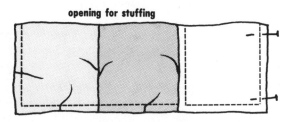

2 Sew the entire "snake" of puffs together, joining the third sides to the first sides in the order already established. It is not important that the pleats meet exactly at the centers of the seams.

Stuffing the Puffs. Stuff the puffs using about $2/3$ cup stuffing (lightly-packed, brown-sugar style). Measure a few times until you "get the feel" of the proper amount, then simply fill the puffs as you see fit. Notice how easy it is to stuff the puff-snake when the puffs have been joined in this fashion.

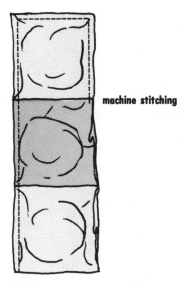

machine stitching

Stitching the Fourth Sides. It may seem that a zipper foot would be best suited for this step, but you would be wise to use the regular presser foot. The left half of the presser foot is needed to keep the puffed fabric out of the way of the needle. With the right sides of the puffs facing you, stitch the fourth sides in one long, continuous seam, pleating as you go.

Winding and Pinning the Wreath. The winding process will be simpler if you begin at the middle of the snake and work toward the ends. The long snake is too unwieldy to pull repeatedly through the center of the styrofoam form.

Place the middle red puff on the front side of the wreath at the top. Grasp the wreath in your left hand, holding the red puff in place with your thumb. Gather up the upper loose end of the snake in your right hand and wrap it around the form and push it through the center. As you wrap the tube, shift the puffs to bring the red puffs and the fifth position green puffs into proper place on the front of the wreath. Wrap both ends of the snake onto the styrofoam form. Shift the puffs closer together or farther apart to use the space evenly. The two free puff ends should meet nicely. Extra puffs may be added after the puffs are secured with pins if they are needed to fill the gap. These extra puffs should simply be pinned in place.

Begin at the top of the wreath, at the center red puff. Pin from the top of the wreath to the bottom on one side, then return to the top and work the other way. Line up the puffs so that the seams joining the puffs together lie together. Turn one seam allowance under and secure it over the seam allowance of the adjoining puff with pins dipped in glue. If you are using colored, plastic-headed pins, you will have the advantage of matching the pins to the fabric.

The extreme fullness of the puffs in the inside curve of the wreath makes pinning unnecessary. Simply tuck under the seam allowances. The number of pins needed to secure the puffs to the outer curve of the wreath will depend upon the fullness of the puffs.

If the place where the two ends of the snake meet is a little messy, never fear. A bow will be affixed there!

Bias Bow.

SMALL BOW: Tied, this bow occupies about an 8″ square space. Finished, it is approximately 34″ in length. Cut a 6″ strip of fabric, 44/45″ wide, from selvage to selvage. Trim off the selvages. Lay the strip

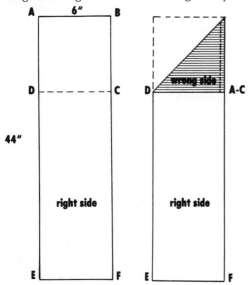

of fabric vertically on the table, with the 6″ sides at the top and bottom. Right side up, fold the left-hand corner A down to point C, forming a triangle. Sew a ¼″ seam starting at point B, ending ¼″ above the combined point A and C. Lift the presser foot and pivot only the top layer of fabric so that A-D-E edge lies along the C-F edge. Lower the presser foot and stitch ¼″ from the edge. The fabric will bunch up, but never fear. Halfway down the side, leave a 2″ opening for turning. Stop stitching ¼″ from point F (it will be on the bottom layer of fabric). Lift the presser foot and pivot to sew the E-F end of the fabric closed. If the ends do not meet to form a nice edge from F to E, the fabric probably was not square. If the discrepancy is not too great (less than ½″ off), sew whatever you need to make a point. If the discrepancy *is* great, it would be best to start over with a fresh piece of fabric.

LARGE BOW: This bow will have approximately 44″ of tying length. Cut a 9″ strip of fabric, 1½ widths of 44/45″ fabric. Trim the selvages and sew the half width to the full width in a ¼″ seam to yield a piece of fabric 9″ by 66″. Make the bow in the same manner as the small bow.

TWO-TONE BOW: Cut 5″ strips of two fabrics, each 1½ widths of 44/45″ fabric. Sew the half widths to the full widths of each color. Then join the two colors along their long edges to form a piece of fabric 9½″ by 66″. Consider the entire unit as a single piece and make the bow as you would a small bow. The two colors do not appear as the front and back of the bow. Instead, they spiral in alternation, barber-pole style.

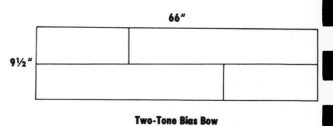

Two-Tone Bias Bow

How to Tie the Bow. This sure-fire method has one drawback: it requires 2 people. Enlist the help of the nearest person who should extend her (his!) index fingers 8″ apart in front of you.

Place the bow fabric behind the fingers, with the approximate center of the fabric offset 2″ to the right.

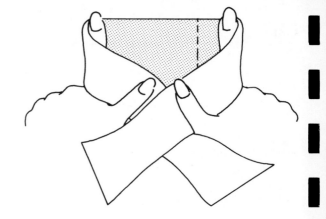

Your friend is looking at the right side of the bow. Bring the tails of the bow around the fingers toward you and cross them in an "X", with the larger right tail on the top. Bring the right tail (now on the left) under the bow front, behind it, and back over the top. Simply tie the two ends together. Surprise!

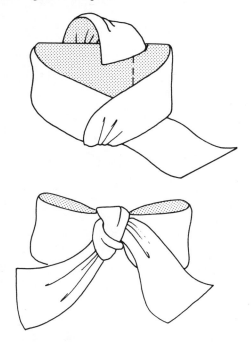

Finishing the Wreath. Make a thread loop or fasten a plastic ring at the top of the backside for hanging. Secure the bias bow to the bottom of the wreath with corsage pins dipped in glue.

Harvest Wreath

Make this wreath using 8 fabrics, either browns, tans, pumpkins, and rusts, or a combination of all of these. Choose a dominant fabric (dominant due to its hue, value, or intensity) and use it in place of the red fabric in the Christmas wreath pattern. Attach wheat, artificial leaves, or miniature cattails beneath the bow for a festive door decoration for the autumn season.

Puff-Patch Pillow

If you have experimented with both the traditional hand method of making and joining puffs and the machine method, you should be well equipped to choose a method or combination of methods for making a pillow. The hot pad-sized puff will yield a 10" to 12" pillow, either in a random fabric arrangement, or perhaps in the design Sunshine and Shadow (5 squares × 5 squares = 25 squares total).

A combination of hand and machine techniques would be the most advantageous. The puff tops should be cut by the mass-cutting technique, with no stitching lines marked. The puff bottoms, however, should be marked on the stitching line (template 1¾" square), and cut by our usual method, *carefully allowing* a ¼" seam. Sew the puff top and bottoms together with the marked stitching line showing on the bottom, using the machine method. Sew puffs in "snakes" one row long. When you join the puffs to each other, follow the stitching line using the machine; ease to make the sides match. The puffs will all be the same size now, with any irregularities pushed into the unimportant seam allowance. The rows will then be joined together, matched, and pinned by the usual method, so that square corners meet nicely. A zipper foot would be advantageous at this step, because the puffs are right side down. If the stitching which created the puffs was in a narrow enough seam, none of this stitching will be visible on the right side.

Warning: Avoid the tendency to overstuff your first pillow.

Puff-Patch Coverlet

By the time you had completed your long snake of puffs for the wreath, you had sewn enough puffs of that size for 3 or 4 rows of a coverlet. Less stuffing should be used in the puffs of the coverlet to facilitate easy joining of rows. If the rows were to be joined as they were in the hot pad, the back of the puff-patch top would be a conglomeration of raw edges. A lining the size of the puffed top should be made and joined to the top as the pillow backing would be joined to a pillow top. It would also be possible to simply baste a lining to the top, wrong sides together, and to finish the raw edges of the top with a binding. In either case, it would be necessary to attach the lining to the top by tacking them together periodically.

A more tedious but very "finished" method can produce a puffed coverlet with a reversible backing. The backing could simply be a fancy fabric used on all the puffs, or could repeat the fabric arrangement of the puffs themselves. No lining would be added, and there would be no need for tacking. To do this, the puffs should be made with the *right side of the top fabric and the right side of the backing together.* After 3 sides have been pleated and stitched, the puff is turned right side out before stuffing. After stuffing, the seam allowances on the fourth side are turned inside, and the opening is blindstitched closed. The finished squares must be blindstitched together. If one fabric is used for all of the puff backs, the coverlet will have a solid fabric backing. If, however, each puff is backed with fabric that matches its puff top, the back of the coverlet would have the same pattern as the puff top.

A coverlet made with puffs of the wreath size would need 20 x 20 puffs (400 total) to yield an approximately 75" square coverlet.

UNIT VII
Cathedral and Attic Window

Like the puff-patch, this is not actually a quilting project, but it is included as an interesting form of piece-work. Unbleached muslin is always used as the background fabric, because it folds and creases well and because of its low thread count. Squares of muslin are precisely folded and refolded into smaller multilayered squares which are then joined. A smaller, printed square is set half-and-half on two adjacent muslin squares. The folded edges of the muslin, which are bias, are stitched over the raw edges of the printed square. The low thread count of the muslin makes its bias extremely stretchy and cooperative. The overall effect is one of diamonds in circles.

While this may seem an inefficient use of fabric, no batting or quilt backing is needed. The finished product is a thing of overwhelming beauty, well worth the time and expense. Cathedral window is called "attic window" if large squares are used. What constitutes "large" or "small" I'm not sure.

The nature of Cathedral Window makes the addition of borders impossible. The design flows exactly to the edge of the unit, leaving no seam allowances for joining. A frame for the "window" is most easily created by appliqueing the entire multilayered unit to a square of border fabric. For the purposes of explanation, this border will be referred to as the "applique background." A quilt made of cathedral window squares would not be appliqued in any way, of course.

Unbleached muslin has a thread count of 60 to 80 threads per inch. You should purchase 100 percent cotton, if possible, because it folds and creases so nicely. If 100 percent cotton is not available, purchase whatever blend you can find. If your fabric comes out of the dryer sorely needing ironing, reject it, and purchase something else. After you have mastered the technique using muslin, you may experiment with colored 100 percent cotton for a novel effect.

Some Options in Cathedral Window Pillows. If you do not like the border of empty half-diamonds on the edge of the unit, you may cut 12 more panes from Fabric B. These may be inserted in the muslin spaces by stitching curves on 2 sides and folding the excess pane fabric to the backside and basting it in place.

If the outer edge of the window unit is not even enough to suit you, you may applique a decorative ribbon over the junction of the window and the border-applique.

Cathedral Window Pillow
16" Pillow (includes 2" border on all sides)

Materials

7/8 yd. unbleached muslin, 100 percent cotton, 36" or 45" wide

1/8 yd. Fabric A, for "panes"

1/8 yd. Fabric B, for "panes"

1/2 yd. Fabric A or B for applique background and pillow backing

Polyester filling

Decorative edging

Templates. Cut 1 square of cardboard *exactly* 8" square. The accuracy of this template is the secret to successful Cathedral Windows. You may cut the 9" squares of muslin freehand. The seam allowances will be ironed over the template to form precision 8" squares.

The second template should be 2 3/4" square. It will be used to cut the "panes." This is the actual cut size — do not leave additional seam allowances.

Cutting

Unbleached muslin	9	9" squares
Fabric A	4	2 3/4" squares
Fabric B	8	2 3/4" squares
Fabric A or B		17" applique background
Fabric A or B		17" pillow backing

Folding Procedure. As in Origami paper folding, the neatness of the finished product depends entirely upon the precision of the original square. Cathedral Window is fascinatingly simple if steps #1 and #2 are done properly. If not, nothing can ever be done to really correct the situation.

1 Cut the 8″ square cardboard template with accuracy. Deviation of 1/16″ could cause problems in the folding process.

2 Lay a 9″ muslin square on the ironing board. Place the cardboard square in the center of the muslin, leaving a ½″ seam allowance all around. You needn't be too picky about centering the cardboard — it's the 8″ square that matters, not the perfection of the seam allowances. Fold the top ½″ and the bottom ½″ over the cardboard and iron the seam allowances in place. Fold over and iron the ½″ seam allowances on the sides. Remove the cardboard. Ignoring the folded-in seam allowances, fold the 8″ muslin squares into perfect (!) fourths, and iron the folds for future reference. Prepare all 9 muslin squares.

cardboard

3 With right sides together, fold a square in half, matching the corners carefully. Fasten with a pin if you like, but eventually you will discover that you can stitch accurately without pinning. You will blindstitch the right- and left-hand edges from the top to a point 2¼″ down from the top. It is not necessary to measure the 2¼″ on each side. Simply fold the fabric again lengthwise and crease the fabric at the seam allowance to indicate the midpoint of the side. Stitch from a point ½″ or so below the midpoint up to the corner on one side. It is difficult to explain

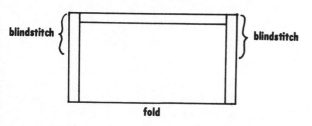

blindstitch   blindstitch

fold

why this peculiar measuring and stitching is recommended now. As you examine the completed muslin square, you will understand.

4 Sew the opposite side in the same manner.

5 Turn the muslin piece right side out and lay it on the table so that the two seams meet at the center, making a smaller square. The original 4 corners should meet *exactly* at the intersection of your ironed-in creases. Smooth the square flat with your fingers. Crease the outer edges (which are bias) with your thumbnail.

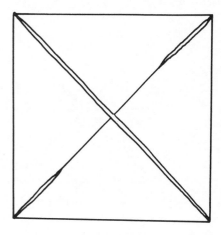

6 Rotate the square on the table, if necessary, so that the seams point north and south. You will now stitch an east-west seam. Fold the upper ½ of the diamond back behind the lower half. Beginning 1½″ from the right-hand edge, blindstitch the seam to a point 1½″ from the left-hand edge. Use caution that you do not

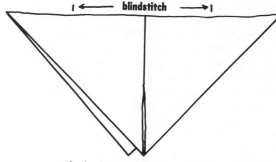

blindstitch

catch the backing fabric into the stitching as you make this seam. Pull the top layer away from the backing after you have stitched to be certain that the backing is free. Lay the square flat on the table. It should measure approximately 5⅝″ square. This completes folding phase #1.

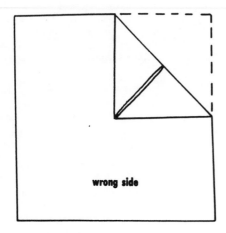

wrong side

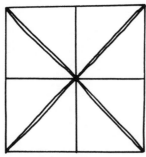

7 Turn the square over so that a smooth piece of fabric is facing you. Fold the 4 corners to the center. The creases will indicate exactly where that center is. Stitch the 4 corners neatly together. Tack the top to the bottom layer through the junction of the 4 corners. The bottom will have 4 stitched seams forming an "X". The right side has a total of 16 folded edges radiating from the center. The completed square should measure nearly 4″ square. This completes folding phase #2.

It should be clear now why you have stitched about ¹/₂″ in excess of halfway on those first seams. The knots are now on the right side of the square. These knots will be concealed by the panes in the finished product. Stitching less than this far would have left knots and gaps on the underside of the quilt, never to be concealed. Stitching farther beyond the midpoint would not enhance the finished product, but would waste time and effort. Fold and stitch all nine muslin squares.

Joining the Squares. Place 2 squares wrong sides together, and blindstitch along one side. It does not matter which 2 edges of the 2 squares are joined, because the edges are all identical. Join a third square to form a row of 3.

Join the remaining 6 squares into rows of 3. Then join the rows together to form a 3-square x 3-square piece, measuring approximately 11³/₄″.

Inserting the Window Panes. Place the muslin unit on the table right side up (stitched seams down). You should see 4 large diamonds in the center. Place your Fabric A panes on these 4 muslin diamonds to check proper placement. It is important to note that the position of the panes is half on one muslin square and half on the adjoining square. Place the Fabric B panes on the muslin to convince yourself that all is going well. Stitch the panes in place:

1 Pin the first A pane in place. Temporarily remove the other panes.

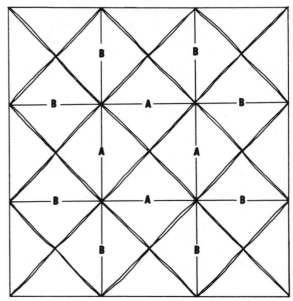

2 Turn under the raw edge ever so slightly on one side of A, and fold the edge of the muslin diamond in a smooth curve over the pane. The curve is bias. It is not difficult to do this properly — only so much of the muslin can be folded over before the entire diamond begins to be distorted.

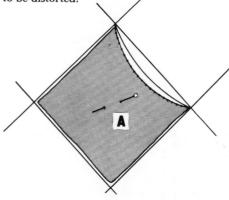

3 Notice that you can slip your finger between the curved fold and the backing. Working against the fingers of your left hand, pin the curved edge in place. Pin the other 3 curves; keeping the backing free.

4 Lightly blindstitch the curves into place. For the last ¼″ of the curves, stitch adjoining curves together for a very crisp look.

5 Continue adding panes until the window is finished.

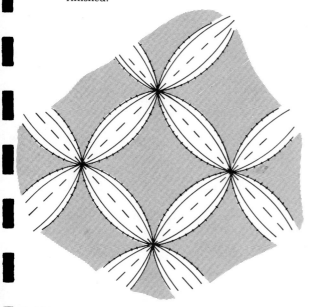

Finishing. Applique the "window" to the applique background. Finish the pillow as desired.

Knowing When to Worry. If your original square was indeed square, all of your corners should have been pointed and crisp as you folded and refolded. Until you gain experience, it is very difficult to know when a square is too far wrong to be acceptable, how to correct problems, and how to hide knots. It is recommended that you work several squares as best you can to familiarize yourself with the technique. Then you may begin to devise your own methods of hiding knots and eliminating gaps at the corners. A few basic pointers may help:

1 Usually 3 corners will be beautiful, and the fourth will show a small gap. If this gap is 1/16″ or less, roll and crease the outer edge of the square to create a crisper point, easing the excess toward the center. A gap which is greater could be the result of a bad template or sloppy ironing. Discard the square, or hope to fix the problem when the muslin squares are joined (maybe!).

2 You will notice that many knots will be concealed under the panes and needn't be hidden during the stitching process.

3 Notice that blindstitching enables you to lay the muslin squares flat in the finished product. Overcasting the folded edges would create little ridges in the squares. Conventional seaming, inside-out, would be difficult.

4 To neatly conceal the stitches in the final fold process on a square, stitch as follows:

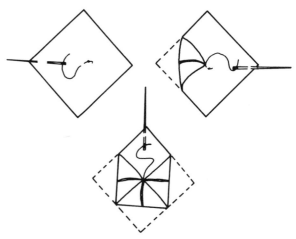

a Begin step #7 of the folding process with the square wrong side up (no seams). Take a ⅛″ stitch in the middle of the square, through one layer only. Take a stitch at one point, beginning ⅛″ in from the point and coming out exactly at the point. As the thread is pulled taut, the corner will be pulled into place.

b Insert the needle exactly at the center and take a ⅛″ stitch toward a second corner. Take a stitch at the corner. Pull the stitch taut and the corner into place.

c Stitch the remaining 2 corners.

d Neatly blindstitch the points together for extra security.

e Run the needle to the backside and end the thread by backstitching in the seams.

5 As you join square to square, you may find some discrepancy in size or minor gaps at corners. To correctly match squares, imagine where the exact corner *should be* and join the squares there, instead of at the actual corner.

6 The point at which 4 muslin squares meet will be the junction of 4 panes as well. It will show in the finished product and must be neatly matched and stitched.

7 If you ever change the size of your initial muslin square, remember to sew ½″ beyond the midpoint on the sides. This will always put the knots on the right side where they will be concealed by panes.

8 If the original 8″ square is lopsided ⅛″ or more, or if the ironing is inaccurate, you will have difficulty disguising the problem.

9 If the muslin is slightly off-grain and can't be straightened, it will still work well.

Chapter 1/Designing Your Quilt

It happens to all of us! By the time a quilter has a set of three pillows on the sofa, the husband (or mother, sister, or meddling neighbor) cannot withstand the urge to comment, "Well, I can see you've got the 'hang' of pillows — when do we see the quilt?" Shame on them all. They consider only the finished product and miss the thrill of the "making."

Actually, after you have successfully pieced two rows of squares together, you are competent enough to piece an entire Sunshine and Shadow quilt. After Simple Star has been mastered, virtually any pattern consisting of squares and triangles is within your capability. The hex on hexagons is undone after you have pieced one flower, so a Flower Garden quilt is ready to blossom. The same can be said for piecing curves. Even circular or intricate applique designs can be undertaken. Technique is no longer the question. Determining fabric requirements, balancing colors and design, and finding the time are the challenges.

Pillows, placemats, and wall hangings are fine, up to a point, but a full-sized quilt compounds the rewards. As one puts a quilt top on the frame, the feeling of accomplishment is replaced by one of expectation. One finds a quiet peace as she sits in front of a frame, with the rhythmic pull on the needle after each set of stitches. There is an indescribable elation in that last stitch. Finally the great plan becomes a reality.

Frame quilting *is* different from lap-quilting. Once you have made the adjustment, you will probably prefer the frame. If space is really a problem, you may continue lap-quilting indefinitely, creating complex designs with elaborate latticework and borders and thousands of tiny pieces, so long as the basic units are rectangular or square. Whichever method you prefer, do not measure your creation in terms of time; measure it, instead, in enjoyment and pride.

Pattern Selection. Is this project something to satisfy a temporary need — a baby quilt, an oversized door decoration for the holidays? Pick a design that is large and has few pieces. Is this a once-in-a-lifetime gift for a sister or mother in appreciation for a lifetime of devotion? Then certainly you will not hesitate to undertake a labor of love. If you aren't certain about the degree of difficulty of a pattern, try making a pillow or sampler first.

Dozens of patterns have been diagrammed throughout the book. In addition to these, any one of the following patterns would be a good choice for the experienced beginner. The patterns which require drafting are included for the more advanced beginner.

Table A indicates which size templates should be used to yield 12", 14" and 16" blocks. The templates can be made from the permanent template section.

Table A. **Guide for Template and Block Sizes**

	12" block	14" block	16" block
Anvil	3" □ and △		4" □ and △
Bear Tracks (alias Bear Claws, Bear's Paw, Duck's Foot-in-the-Mud, Hand of Friendship, Cross and Crown, Goose Tracks and Bear's Foot)			2" □ and △ 4" □ 2" x 4" ▭
Clay's Choice (alias Jackson's Star, Harry's Star, Henry of the West, Star of the West)	3" □ and △		4" □ and △
Dutchman's Puzzle (alias Wind Mill)	3" △		4" △
Drunkard's Path and variations	3" templates		4" templates
Hen and Chickens		2" □ and △ 2" x 6" ▭ 4" □	
Sailboat (alias Mayflower)	3" □ and △		4" □ and △
Pierced Star (alias Barbara Frietchie Star)	3"△		4"△
Robbing Peter to Pay Paul (our version)	2" □ and △ 2" x 4" ▭ 4" □		
Simple Star (alias Evening Star)	3" □ and △ 6" □		

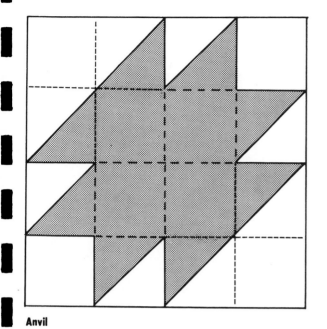

Anvil

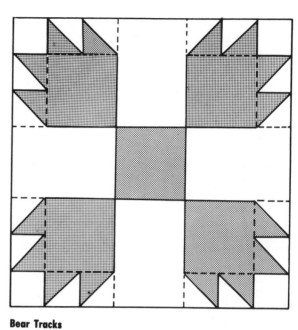

Bear Tracks

Clay's Choice

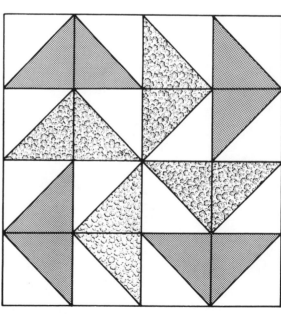

Dutchman's Puzzle

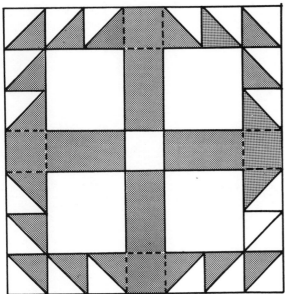

Hen and Chickens

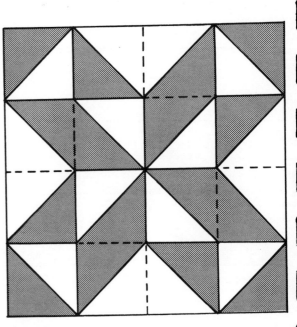

Sailboat

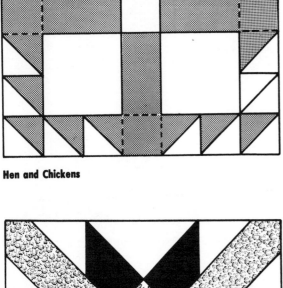

Mexican Star

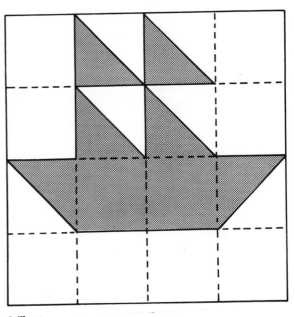

Pierced Star

Oak Leaf

Kentucky Rose

Wreath of Pansies

Hen and Chickens without Lattice

Hen and Chickens with Lattice

Overall Design. The decision to include latticework in a quilt must be a carefully deliberated one. Lattice strips can effectively break the monotonous repetition of a pattern, causing the eye to focus on the basic unit. It can, on the other hand, interrupt the gentle flow of the design. At its worst, it can overwhelm the viewer's attention, defeating its purpose.

Graph paper and colored pencils offer a good means to experiment with latticework and color. Any square or rectangular design can be set in lattice strips, and the latticework can be simple or elaborate.

A very simple design can look very different when a lattice strip separates the blocks. The coloring and size of an elaborate lattice system can greatly affect the depth of a quilt design. As a rule of thumb, the less eye-catching the lattice fabric, the wider the strips may be without overpowering the blocks.

Some patterns form a pseudo-lattice structure on their own. Mexican Star forms diagonal "lattice strips," while blocks of Hen and Chickens form horizontal-vertical strips. Fabric selection is especially important in these designs as you minimize or maximize this effect. The use of more than two fabrics in such patterns enables the quilter to dramatically control the focal point of the quilt.

Other patterns are lost completely without latticework. Blocks of Grandmother's Favorite conjunctively form a secondary star design, very similar to Dolly Madison's Star. Using a different fabric in each block will eliminate this effect and the need for lattice.

To experiment most easily, draw 6 or 8 repeats of the block on graph paper. Cut out the blocks. Try a variety of arrangements on both light and dark backgrounds to become aware of the different effects latticework can achieve. Experiment with narrow and wide lattice. If a copying machine is available, make several copies of a 4 x 6 block unit. Using colored pencils, test the effects of using 3 or more colors and of reversing the colors from one block to the next. You may also experiment by rotating every other block if the pattern is asymmetrical. Cutting out actual-sized pieces from gift wrapping paper is another useful technique.

The colors and designs of the paper give good representation of an actual quilt block.

A few helpful hints may be in order. Generally, the width of the latticework should be no more than ¼ the width of the block. If the color of the lattice is extremely eye-catching (including white), a narrower lattice would be better. Avoid intricate pieced latticework for now. The most important aspect of your first quilt is getting it on the frame and quilted! Deluxe lattice and borders should be reserved for quilts further down the way.

Dolly Madison

Grandmother's Favorite

UNIT VIII
Chapter 2/The Mathematics
of Design

Determining the Size of the Quilt. For your convenience, Table B is given to indicate the mattress dimensions of the four most common standard sizes.

TABLE B. Mattress Dimensions

Size	Width	Length	Thickness	Distance from top to floor
Twin	39″	75″	7″	22″
Full	54″	75″	7″	22″
Queen	60″	80″	7″	22″
King	76″	80″	7″	22″

If your quilt will be used simply as a blanket (tucked in on three sides), you will need to know the thickness of the mattress (call this number M). If you plan to use a dust ruffle with your quilt-coverlet, you will need to measure the distance from the top of the mattress to the top of the dust ruffle (call this number D). If the quilt is to cover the side rail, but not reach the floor, measure the distance from the top of the mattress to the bottom of the side rail (call this number S). If you plan to make a full bedspread, measure from the top of the mattress to the floor or rug, if it is very thick (call this number F). If you plan to tuck the quilt under the pillows, add 12-18″ to the length.

Because quilting "takes up" or shrinks the finished size, the quilt top should be larger than the desired size of the finished quilt. For beginners, this amount is generally 3 to 5 percent of the desired size. This is the result of a slight "gathering" effect of the quilting. As your stitching improves, you will find that it is possible for the stitches to hold the layers together (up and down tension) without puckering the fabric, even ever so slightly (sideways tension). To illustrate the way to compensate for this shrinking, suppose you are planning a quilt which should be 100″ x 100″. Cut the pieces and borders as though you were making a 105″ x 105″ quilt (5% allowance). After quilting, the quilt should be approximately 100″ x 100″. This allowance is the shrinkage factor (SF). It is most critical if the quilt must meet a dust ruffle or conceal a side rail. Otherwise, you may simply choose to ignore the calculation, which usually amounts to no more than 3″ or 4″.

The average shrinkage factor is about 5 percent. If you feel the need for more precision, determine your own personal shrinkage factor. By measuring several of your pillows (minus borders) and calculating the theoretical size by measuring the templates, you can determine the shrinkage. For instance, the theoretical size of the pieced portion of Drunkard's Path is 11″. Suppose your block is 10½″. Divide the actual size by the theoretical size (10.5 ÷ 11 = 0.95). Your project is 95 percent of the theoretical size; your shrinkage factor is 5 percent.

It is not always wise to size a quilt too specifically for one bed. The size of the block and the decision to use or not to use lattice set certain limitations on sizing. People often "doctor" the size of the top by adding borders of different widths to the sides and ends of the top. If absolute precision is necessary, you may do this, but an evenly designed quilt is usually prettier.

Sometimes a plain strip 12″ to 18″ wide is added between the first and second horizontal rows if the quilt is to be tucked under pillows. This saves the time required to piece or applique an additional row, but if time is so valuable, it would be better to enlarge the design by 2″ per block. Only if the top is an album design, each block being unique, is this shortcut really justified. I agree that it would be a shame to make a row of individual masterpieces which would never be seen. An even better solution than adding the "plain row" to an album quilt would be to rotate the quilt on the bed from time to time, giving the viewer a fresh perspective.

To estimate the desired size of the quilt, calculate the width and length using the measurements you have made and the formulas in Table C.

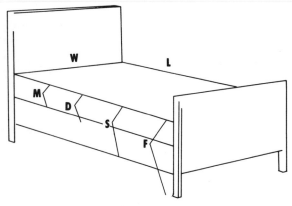

Diagram of required measurements

W = width of mattress

L = length of mattress

M = thickness of mattress

F = distance from top of mattress to floor or rug

D = distance from top to dust ruffle

S = distance from top to bottom of side rail

SF = shrinkage factor

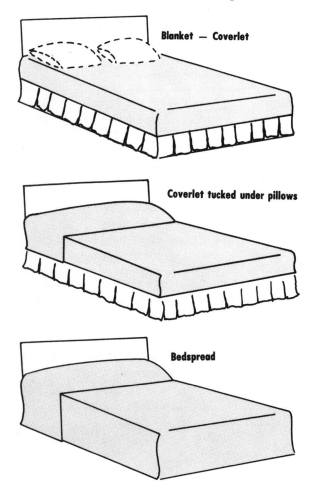

Blanket — Coverlet

Coverlet tucked under pillows

Bedspread

Table C. Formulas for Determining Quilt Sizes

Quilt Type	Width	Length
Blanket-coverlet (4″ tuck allowance)	W + 2M + 8″ + SF	L + 1M + 4″ + SF
Coverlet, to dust ruffle (4″ overhang)	W + 2D + 8″ + SF	L + 1D + 4″ + SF
Coverlet, tucked under pillows	W + 2M + 8″ + SF	L + 1M + 4″ + 18″ + SF
Coverlet, tucked under pillows, to dust ruffle	W + 2D + 8″ + SF	L + 1D + 4″ + 18″ + SF
Bedspread, tucked under pillows nearly reaching the floor	W + 2F + SF	L + 1F + 18″ + SF
Bedspread, tucked under pillows and reaching the bottom of the side rails (2″ overhang)	W + 2S + 4″ + SF	L + 1S + 2″ + 18″ + SF

After you have added the measurements for the mattress and overhang in any of the six styles, multiply the total by your SF percentage. Add this amount to the first total. These dimensions are the *theoretical size* of the quilt. Example: Suppose you are planning a queen-sized bedspread, tucked under the pillows, with a distance to the floor of 22″. The calculations would be as follows:

$$
\begin{array}{cc}
\text{WIDTH} & \text{LENGTH} \\
\text{W} + 2\text{F} + \text{SF (5\%)} & \text{L} + 1\text{F} + 18'' + \text{SF (5\%)} \\
60'' + 44'' + \text{SF} & 80'' + 22'' + 18'' + \text{SF} \\
104'' + (104 \times 0.05 = 5'') & 120'' + (120 \times 0.05 = 6'') \\
109'' \quad\quad \text{x} & 126''
\end{array}
$$

It would be understandable if you would choose to decrease the width by a few inches so that the quilt would not drag on the floor if your estimates and measurements were too generous.

Use the mathematical formula to check your understanding of the method of calculation. You may check your results against some of the figures in Table D.

Table D shows estimated sizes for the three most common styles of quilts in four sizes. Standard mattress sizes were used in the calculations. The bedspread will hang 2″ above the floor, if the top of the mattress is the standard 22″ from the floor. *The allowance for shrinkage has not been included in this table.*

Table D. Dimensions for the Most Common Quilt Styles in Four Standard Sizes

Size	Mattress Dimensions	Blanket-Coverlet	Coverlet, Tucked Under Pillows	Bedspread, Tucked Under Pillows
Twin	39″ x 75″	61″ x 86″	61″ x 104″	79″ x 113″
Full	54″ x 75″	76″ x 86″	76″ x 104″	94″ x 113″
Queen	60″ x 80″	82″ x 91″	82″ x 109″	100″ x 118″
King	76″ x 80″	98″ x 91″	98″ x 109″	116″ x 118″

Determining the Number of Blocks. For any pattern which is used without latticework, divide the theoretical width of the quilt (including SF) by the width of the quilt block to determine the number of blocks in a horizontal row. Divide the theoretical length of the quilt (including SF) by the length of the quilt block to determine the number of blocks in a vertical row. Rarely are these results even numbers. You may enlarge the dimensions of the quilt to permit the use of whole blocks, or you may add a border to the blocks. If the required borders on the sides and top-bottom edges do not match, use the larger number. Of course this amount of border must be divided by 2, half of the total for each side.

If lattice is to be added, the figuring becomes slightly more complex. If you have taken the time to estimate a few quilt sizes by the formulas in Table C, you surely have realized that there is considerable room for guess-work. The method of calculation is an important one to understand, but for general purposes, this second, simplified table is much easier to use.

These figures represent finished sizes and no allowance for "shrinkage" has been made. To calculate the length of a coverlet which does tuck under the pillows, simply add 12" to 18" to the lengths for the coverlets without tuck-under.

The easiest way to compute quilt size is to begin adding block-width dimensions to lattice-width dimensions until you near the desired measurement. Divide the remaining portion by 2 and plan the borders that size. Do the same for the lengthwise dimension. Select the larger of the 2 border measurements if they are not the same.

The SF can be used in 2 ways. If the measurement of an even number of blocks exceeds the desired dimensions by 3 to 5 percent, you may use the even number of blocks, not adding borders or additional inches for shrinkage. Otherwise, simply add the 5 percent, usually about 1" to 2" to the borders on all four sides.

Table E. Adjusted Sizes for Quiltmaking

Size	Coverlet, No Tuck-Under width-length	Bedspread, Tuck-Under width-length
Twin	68" x 86"	81" x 110"
Full	76" x 86"	94" x 110"
Queen	92" x 92"	102" x 120"
King	100" x 100"	120" x 120"

Three tables are given to indicate the number of blocks needed to make 4 sizes of quilts in the 3 most common styles. A separate table is given for 12", 14" and 16" blocks with lattice strips approximately ¼ the width of the block. No shrinkage allowance is included. The calculated dimensions of the quilt top are given only so that you can be aware of the necessary deviation from the theoretical sizes.

		BLANKET-COVERLET				COVERLET-TUCKED				BEDSPREAD-TUCKED			
		Number of Blocks width of Quilt	length of Quilt	Border Width	Calculated Size	Number of Blocks width of Quilt	length of Quilt	Border Width	Calculated Size	Number of Blocks width of Quilt	length of Quilt	Border Width	Calculated Size
Table F.	Twin	4 x 6		2"	61"x91"	4 x 7		3"	63"x108"	5 x 7		5"	82"x112"
12" Blocks	Full	5 x 6		2"	76"x91"	5 x 7		3"	78"x108"	6 x 7		5"	97"x112"
with	Queen	5 x 6		5"	82"x97"	5 x 7		5"	82"x112"	7 x 8		—	102"x117"
3" Wide Lattice	King	6 x 6		5"	97"x97"	6 x 7		5"	97"x112"	8 x 8		—	117"x117"
Table G.	Twin	4 x 5		3"	71"x88"	4 x 6		3"	71"x105"	5 x 7		—	87"x116"
14" Blocks	Full	4 x 5		5"	75"x92"	4 x 6		5"	75"x109"	5 x 6		6"	94"x111"
with	Queen	5 x 5		5"	92"x92"	5 x 6		4"	90"x107"	6 x 7		—	99"x116"
3" Wide Lattice	King	6 x 6		—	99"x99"	6 x 6		5"	109"x109"	7 x 7		—	116"x116"
Table H.	Twin	3 x 4		5"	66"x86"	3 x 5		4"	64"x104"	4 x 6		2"	80"x120"
16" Blocks	Full	4 x 4		5"	86"x86"	4 x 5		4"	84"x104"	5 x 6		2"	100"x120"
with	Queen	4 x 5		3"	82"x102"	4 x 5		5"	86"x106"	5 x 6		3"	102"x122"
4" Wide Lattice	King	5 x 5		4"	104"x104"	5 x 5		4"	104"x104"	6 x 6		2"	120"x120"

Correct the size for shrinkage before cutting by adding 1″ to 3″ to the width of all 4 borders. If you have found that your own SF is 2 percent or less, or if the exact size of the finished quilt is not critical, you may omit this step.

Table F indicates that 64 blocks would be needed to make the king-sized bedspread from 12″ blocks. It is no wonder that these large quilts often have 18″ borders of 2, 3, or 4 strips of fabric framing the quilt. The use of this type of border cuts the number of blocks required to a mere 36. If such a large border does not appeal to you, you may choose to enlarge the 12″ block to a 16″ block (36 blocks needed). This is recommended only if the pattern pieces are relatively small. For example, Robbing Peter to Pay Paul (our version) would still be attractive in a 16″ block. Simple Star would be *too* simple.

Alternatives in Border Design. If extremely wide borders are to be used on a quilt, the top border will lie across the exposed pillow area. In such cases, special planning may be necessary. If the quilt is to tuck under pillows, the finished product will have a more professional look if the top and bottom borders are last to be joined, extending the entire width of the quilt plus the width of the 2 side borders. The junction of the borders should be concealed in the folds and would not show when the bed is made.

If the quilt is to be a coverlet with pillow shams, the opposite would be true. The side borders should be the longer borders, extending completely along the side, uninterrupted by seams. The junction of the side and top border would be minimized by the attention-drawing pillow shams.

After you have determined how wide you would like the border to be, determine the length of the border strips as follows:

Top and bottom strips = the width of the completed quilt top, edge to edge

Length of side strips = length of quilt top (before joining the top and bottom borders) + the width of the top border + the width of the bottom border − ½″ (to subtract for seams)

If you plan to miter the corners of the borders, all 4 borders would have to be the length (or width) of the quilt plus the width of 2 borders.

Quilt to be tucked under pillows

Quilt to be used with pillow shams

mitered border

UNIT VIII

Chapter 3/Determining Fabric Requirements

The Mathematical Formula. Many experienced quilters have never mastered this fundamental aspect of *all* handiwork. They will be forever limited to following mass-produced patterns or forced to rely on the quick judgment of a salesclerk who may make a serious, though unintentional, error.

Draw a quick sketch of the quilt, showing the arrangement of blocks, all latticework (strips and squares) and border sections. Itemize the pieces in one block, indicating how many times each piece is used and from which fabric it should be cut.

You are ready to begin determining the fabric required to make your quilt.

Count the number of times a piece is used in each block (this number is N). Multiply N by the number of blocks in the quilt (number of blocks is B) to obtain the total number of the specified piece needed for the entire quilt (this total is T). Divide the width of the preshrunk fabric by the width (w) of the piece being cut, being certain to allow ½″ between the pieces for the seam allowances and a few inches for wasted selvages. This quotient, called W, is the number of pieces you will be able to cut from one width of fabric. W must be a whole number, because a fraction of a pattern piece is of no use. Divide the total number of pieces, T, by W to determine how many widths of fabric you will need to mark and cut all of the pieces of that one type. The number of widths you will need is called R, for "rows." Multiply R by the height (h) of the individual piece being considered (remember seam allowances) to determine how many inches of fabric to buy. Divide this number by 36 to convert to yards.

If more than one type of piece is to be cut from any given fabric, determine the amount needed for each piece and add those amounts together to determine the total yardage required of that fabric.

Calculate the fabric needed for latticework (squares and strips), borders, and binding. If you prefer, you may use the same process to determine the yardage for latticework as you did to determine yardage for the pieces. Borders should be cut in long continuous pieces.

Plan ample fabric for bias binding. The mathematical determinations for one piece are as follows:

N = the number of each particular piece in each block

w = the width of the piece, plus seam allowances

h = the height of the piece, plus seam allowances

B = the number of blocks in the quilt

$N \times B = T$ = the total number of that piece in the entire quilt

W = the number of pieces that can be cut from one width of fabric (obtained by dividing the width of the fabric by w)

$\dfrac{T}{W} = R$ = the number of widths you will need or the number of rows you will need to mark

Y = the total yardage needed; multiply R by h, then divide the product by 36″

In the determination of R and Y, always round numbers to the next highest whole number.

If the piece under consideration is a triangle, diamond, or hexagon, it is very inefficient to consider marking a row of single pieces. It takes very little extra space, for example, to mark a pair of triangles in the place of one. In such cases, figure the number of pieces that fit in this multiple unit and divide T by that number. The dimensions w and h of this unit would then be substituted for the w and h of the single piece in subsequent computations.

If more than one piece is to be cut from a given fabric, remember to add the number of inches required to cut each piece. Then divide this total by 36 to convert inches to yards.

Oftentimes, the lattice squares are omitted and the vertical lattice strip is a continuous piece of fabric between the rows. You may choose to use this time-saving shortcut, or add lattice strips and squares to the blocks individually.

An Exercise in Mathmematics. The problem will be to determine the amount of fabric required for a full-sized quilt-coverlet which will tuck under the pillows. The selected pattern is Bear Tracks. The blocks will be 16" square, set apart by lattice strips 4" wide.

Begin your calculation by determining the dimensions of the quilt using the formula from Table C.

**Determining the Theoretical
Size of the Quilt
And the General Layout**

Width = W + 2M + 8" + SF (3%)
          54" + 14" + 8"   = 76"
          SF = 76" x 0.03   = 2"
                    Total   78"

Length = L + 1M + 4" + 18" + SF (3%)
           75" + 7" + 4" + 18"   = 104"
           SF = 104" x 0.03   = 3"
                     Total   107"

Table H, on page 93, indicates that a quilt of these dimensions, style, and block size should consist of 4 blocks per horizontal row and 5 blocks per vertical row. There will be a total of 20 blocks in the quilt. The next calculation should be the exact border size.

For the width of the quilt there will be 4 blocks set apart by 3 lattice strips. The theoretical width should be 78".

4 blocks x 16"   = 64"
3 lattice strips x 4" = 12"
          Total   76", 2" less than the necessary
                     amount

For the length of the quilt, there will be 5 blocks set apart by 4 lattice strips. The theoretical length should be 107".

5 blocks x 16"   = 80"
4 lattice strips x 4" = 16"
                    96", 11" less than the neces-
                     sary amount

Because there is such a large difference in the amount needed for the side and top-bottom borders. a compromise should be made. The 18" allowed for the tuck-under is very generous. As little as 12" would have been sufficient. Therefore, if the total length were to fall slightly short of 107", no harm should be done. Furthermore, because this is a coverlet and not a bedspread, it would not matter if the sides were to hang a little bit lower. Consequently, we will add 8" to both the width and length as borders. Dividing the amount by 2, the borders should be cut 4" wide. The side borders should be 96" long (the actual size of the quilt top). The top and bottom borders should be the width of the actual top plus the width of 2 borders, or 84" (76" + 4" + 4"). The completed quilt top will measure 84" x 104"

Determining the Fabric Required for the Quilt. After you have planned the basic structure of your quilt, figuring yardage is a matter of simple arithmetic.

Analyzing the Quilt Block

	Piece #	Number of Pieces/Block	Template	Dimensions Actual Cutting size
Fabric A	#1	5	4" x 4"	4½" x 4½"
	#2	16	2"△	2½" x 3" (cuts 2)
Fabric B	#2	16	2"△	2½" x 3" (cuts 2)
	#3	4	2" x 2"	2½" x 2½"
	#4	4	4" x 6"	4½" x 6½"

Analyzing the Latticework, Borders, and Binding

Piece	Number in Quilt	Dimensions Finished	Cut size
Fabric A Lattice strips	31	4" x 16"	4½" x 16½"
Lattice squares	12	4" x 4"	4½" x 4½"
Top-bottom borders	2	4" x 84"	4½" x 84½"
Side borders	2	4" x 96"	4½" x 96½"
Binding		2" x 400"	45" square

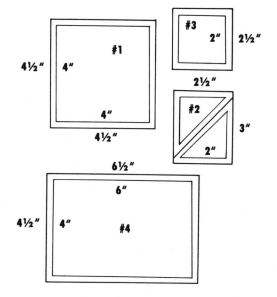

Calculations. To calculate the actual amounts of fabric required, make a table for yourself on a sheet of blank paper. Duplicate the headings and columns of Table I. which follows. Using the data from above, fill in the table. Compare your results with those in Table I. Answers within ¼ yd. are adequate.

Table I: Fabric Requirements

	Piece	Dimensions Cutting Size		$N \times B = T$	W	$\dfrac{T}{W} = R$	$R \times h$	$\dfrac{R \times h}{36} = Y$
		w	h					
Fabric A	#1	4½″ x	4½″	5 x 20 = 100	9	12	54″	81
	#2 (two per unit)*	2½″ x	3″	16 x 20 = 320*	17	9*	27″	$\overline{36}$ = 2¼ yds. A
Fabric B	#2*	2½″ x	3″	16 x 20 = 320*	17	9*	27″	
	#3	2½″ x	2½″	4 x 20 = 80	17	5	13″	99
	#4	4½″ x	6½″	4 x 20 = 80	9	5	59″	$\overline{36}$ = 2¾ yds. B
Fabric A	Borders - Top/ Bottom	4½″ x 84½″		2				
	Borders - Side	4½″ x 96½″		2	97″	2¾ yds. A		
	Lattice Strips	4½″ x 16½″		31	Cut from border			
	Lattice Squares	4½″ x 4½″		12	remnants plus ½ yd.	½ yd. A		
	Binding	2″ x 400″				45″ sq.	1¼ yds. A	

Total Fabric A = 6¾ yds.   Total Fabric B = 2¾ yds.

*Note: Because 2 #2 triangles can be cut from one 2½″ x 3″ space, 160 of these spaces are needed and not the full 320. In the computation of $\dfrac{T}{W}$ = R, 160 is used as W.

To determine the lattice layout, plan first to cut the 4 border strips. In this case, after 4 sections 4½″ wide have been cut, a 26″ wide piece would remain which would be a minimum of 96½″ long. Using the measurement of the lattice strips with seam allowances and 26″ as the width of the fabric, calculate W. Five rows of lattice strips, 5 per row, can be cut from the piece, as well as the 12 lattice squares. An additional ½ yard of fabric would be required for the remaining 6 lattice strips.

It is always advisable to purchase some additional fabric. In this example, 7 yards of Fabric A and 3¼ yards of Fabric B should be ample. Whether you buy more will depend upon your budget and your plans for your scrapbag.

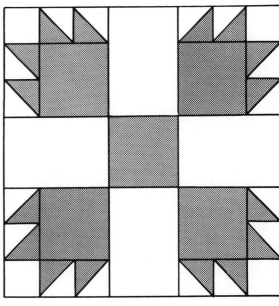

Bear Tracks

UNIT VIII
Chapter 4 / The Quilt Top

Making a Trial Block

The next step is to make a sample block to test the accuracy of the templates and the actual appearance of the fabrics in combination. There are two ways of accomplishing this. For the first, buy a quarter of a yard (more or less) of the required fabrics before the full commitment is made. Complete the trial block. The time wasted in the event of an error in template making or fabric choice would be outweighed by the saving of purchased and wasted fabric. If you are confident of your fabric selection, by all means save yourself a return trip to the store and buy all of the fabric for the quilt at the very beginning.

In either case, *always* make a sample block before you mark all of the fabric. An error in template size or accuracy will quickly be noticed before a small fortune in fabric is marked, cut, and wasted.

Iron as You Go.

How you tackle the enormous job of piecing or appliqueing an entire quilt is up to you. You may choose to piece all of the blocks before you begin the joining process. Instead, you may be eager to "see how it looks," joining blocks as they are completed. Some prefer to complete a row of blocks and join them, then to start anew with the second row. This does seem to be the nicest approach.

In either case, it is suggested that you press the blocks before they are joined, if pressing is required. The conditions under which you work determine how long the blocks will *stay* neatly pressed. Even if a joined row requires some additional ironing, you have spared yourself the tedious and cumbersome job of ironing an entire quilt top in one sitting.

Many people prefer to mark the quilting designs on the blocks before they are joined. Certainly this would require a relatively permanent marker — not powdered bluing, needless to say. This is definitely easier than manipulating the complete top, with the added advantage of subdividing a lengthy chore.

Arranging the Completed Blocks.

If all of the blocks in your quilt are identical, they may be joined as they are completed. If, however, you have made a scrapbag or album quilt, some careful arranging will be necessary.

Lay all of the blocks on a table or on the floor. Rearrange them until you are completely satisfied. For a 16-block quilt, pick up the blocks in the following order: pick up the lower left-hand block, #4; put #3 on top of #4; then #2 and #1; start a second pile with #8 on the bottom and #7, #6, and #5 on top; make similar piles of blocks #12 - #9 and blocks #16 - #13. Pin each group of 4 together. Then, starting with the right-hand row at the bottom, put the 4 rows together. Block #1 should be at the top of the stack.

If latticework is being included, add vertical and horizontal strips and lattice squares following the techniques in the lap-quilting chapter. After the latticework is attached, join the blocks.

Assembling the Blocks.

Blocks of a quilt are assembled in the same manner as squares in a nine-patch. Match all seams, easing if necessary to make the blocks and lattice fit together smoothly.

Borders.

Whether the top-bottom or side borders are the longer of the two, join them in such a way as to avoid creating a right-angle piecing situation. If you are mitering the corners, mark the fabric, recheck the size for proper fit, and then trim away the excess. Join the borders, carefully piecing the 45-degree angles.

Marking the Quilting Designs.

If you have not previously marked the quilting designs on the blocks and lattice, you must do so now. Quilting lines which fall 1/8″ inside piecing lines or along appliques need not be marked.

Carefully study the design of your pattern. Imagine the pattern formed by the quilting stitches as it will appear on the backing, where the fabric and color designs are absent. Adding or eliminating certain lines may create extremely attractive networks of stitches. In Clay's Choice, it would be better *not* to quilt around every piece — on the back the design would be virtually abstract! If only the major shapes were to be quilted, instead, the pinwheel would be duplicated on the backing.

Whatever quilting designs you choose, don't skimp. Often I hear it said that quilters don't quilt like they used to. My answer is an emphatic "Some do!"

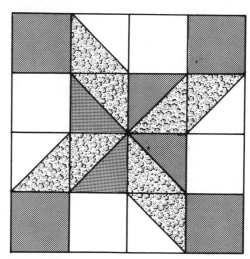

Clay's Choice quilt top

Clay's Choice quilt backing

Quilting every piece

Emphasizing the design

UNIT VIII
Chapter 5/Frame-Quilting

Preparing the Layers. Begin assembling the layers by folding the quilt top. Lay the top on the floor, right side up, smoothing out all of the wrinkles. Fold the right half over onto the left, matching the corners exactly. Mark the fold at the center top and bottom with pins. Now fold the upper quarter down onto the lower quarter, matching the corners and smoothing out the wrinkles. Mark the middle of the sides at the fold by inserting a pin in the left- *and* right-hand sides of the quilt top. With your hand, crease the quilt top along the folds. Lay the quilt top aside.

A generous 4″ excess is necessary on all 4 sides of both the batting and backing. Depending upon the size and style of your quilt, you may or may not need to piece the batting and backing. If it is necessary to add to the width of the backing, avoid running a seam down the center. Divide the additional width in half and add 2 panels, 1 to each side of the center panel. This can be done quickly on the machine. Iron the backing.

Fold, mark and crease the quilt backing in the same manner as the quilt top. Lay it aside.

Cut a piece of batting 4″ larger than the quilt top on all sides. It will be the same size as the quilt backing. If it is necessary to join pieces of batting to obtain the proper size, do so by butting the 2 edges of batting together and seaming them together with large over-casting stitches. Stitch a second time for extra strength. As with the quilt backing, avoid seaming the batting in the center of the quilt top. Do not overlap the edges — lumpy quilts are not fashionable. Quarter-fold the batting and lay it aside.

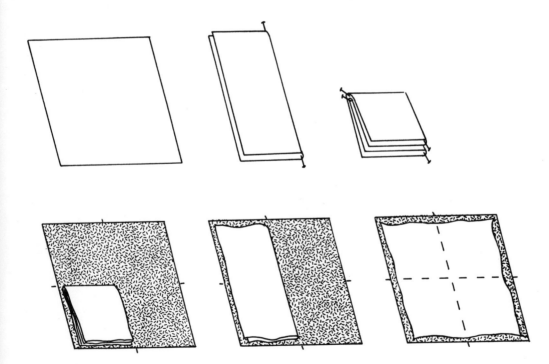

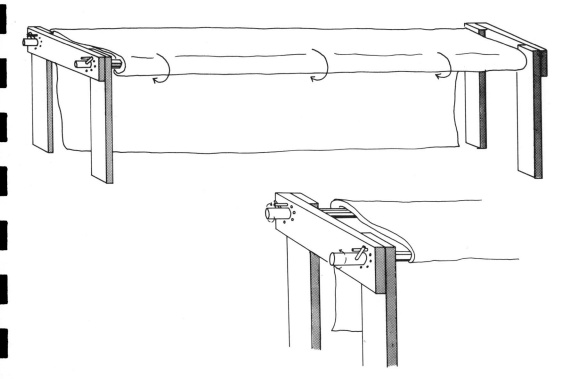

Putting the Quilt on the Frame. If a quilting frame is to be used, two methods of centering the layers are possible. The first is to attach the quilt backing to the fully extended frame before the layers are stacked. The second method is to layer and baste the quilt prior to its attachment to the frame. The second method is the one used to assemble the layers if a small chair frame is to be used.

Begin the first method by setting up the frame according to the manufacturer's instructions, extending it to accommodate the full width and length (if possible) of the quilt. The frame must be large enough to accommodate at least 1 dimension of the quilt. If there are no fabric strips on the stretchers and side rails, you must add them. Strips of muslin, double-thickness, must be stapled to the wood in an even line. The strips may be overlapped if necessary so that the entire width and length of the frame is covered. Either measure or approximate the center of each side.

Beginning at the center on 1 side, and matching the centers of the stretcher and the quilt backing, pin the quilt backing to the ends along that side. Pin the opposite side to its stretcher, pulling the backing taut. Pin the backing to the two side rails.

Unfold the batting and center it on the quilt backing. Do not pull it taut, but do smooth out all of the wrinkles. The batting should extend to the edges of the quilt backing.

Pick up the quilt top. Place the double-folded top in the lower left-hand corner of the quilt backing, matching the creases at the left side middle pin and the bottom middle pin. The quilt top should lie 4″ in from the edges of the backing and the batting. Open the quilt top to half-size, matching the creases at the top pins. Carefully unfold the quilt top to its extended size, matching the creases at the right-hand middle. There must be excess batting and backing on all 4 sides of the quilt top.

Smooth the 3 layers to remove lumps and wrinkles. Any lump not eliminated now will remain in the finished product. Pin-baste the layers together, beginning at the center and pinning every 2″ to 3″. Pinning is easiest with the left hand beneath the quilt, both to apply pressure and to smooth the backing. Reach as far into the center as you possible can, constantly smoothing the fabric toward the outer edges. The pins are less likely to snag or poke if they are inserted parallel to the stretchers.

After the quilt is pinned thoroughly, you may roll the quilt scroll-fashion onto the stretchers to minimize the space it requires. To do so, you must remove the pins from the side rails. Roll half of the quilt onto each stretcher, applying even pressure as you turn the quilt so that there is no distortion of the layers. If the quilt is not "square" on the frame, it will not be square on the bed. Additional pins may be added to the exposed area. Repin the quilt to the side rails. On most frames the extensions of the side rails can be removed and stored.

101

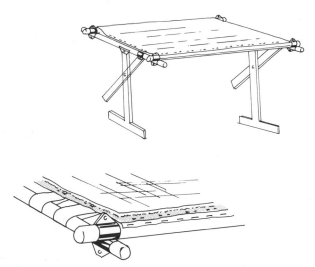

Small Frames. If your frame will not accommodate the entire length of the quilt, or if a hoop or chair-side frame is to be used, stack and center the layers on the floor and pin or baste them thoroughly. Begin by unfolding the backing on the floor, right side down. Unfold the batting and center it on the backing. Do not pull it taut, but do smooth out all of the wrinkles. The batting should extend to the edges of the quilt backing. Unfold the quartered top on the 2 layers, matching the centers of all 4 sides.

Begin pinning at the center, pinning every 2″ to 3″, being certain that the quilt top is not distorted in any way. Actually you may choose to baste the layers together and remove all pins if a chair-side frame is to be used. Baste through all of the thicknesses in rows radiating from the center.

On large-sized projects it will be difficult to slip your left hand under the fabric to facilitate pinning. Learn to pin one-handed, pushing against the floor, checking that each pin is free of the rug by lifting the quilt slightly off the floor before securing the pin.

If a small hoop or other chair-side frame is to be used, you should begin quilting at the center, working outward.

If you plan to use the full-sized frame, but it will not extend to accommodate the entire quilt for securing purposes, center and baste the layers on the floor. Centering the middle of one side of the quilt on the stretcher, pin the first side in place. Carefully roll the quilt onto the stretcher until only enough quilt is left to reach the opposite stretcher. Pin the second side to its stretcher. Roll half of the quilt onto the second stretcher so that the center of the quilt is in the exposed portion. Quilt from the center of the quilt toward one end; then reroll and quilt toward the other end.

The Quilting Stitch. Begin the quilting at the right-hand side if you are right-handed. Frame quilting is easiest if the left hand is beneath the quilt. The point of the needle should glance off the fingernail of the left index or middle finger, signalling the penetration of the needle through all of the layers. The trick is to stop the needle just as it touches the nail, hopefully not after it jabs the fingertip. In frame quilting, the right arm rotates at the elbow to bring the needle back to the top — the wrist is relatively stationary. The right hand does all of the work. Compare this to lap-quilting, in which the left hand and right hand together work both the needle and the fabric simultaneously.

Do not use the needlepoint method of pushing the needle down with the right hand, returning it from underneath with the left. Not only is the process slow, it usually assures a very sloppy backing. Eventually you will be able to take 3 or 4 quilting stitches on the needle all at once.

Yes, you are going to poke your finger once or twice. Fortunately, the blood will usually be on the backing. A germy but surefire stain remover is the quilter's own saliva, dabbed on the spot immediately. This may sound terribly unsanitary, but it really works! Remember, it may be months before the quilt will be off the frame for a soaking in the washing machine with a laundry additive.

More than one quilter has asked if a thimble can be worn on the left index finger to prevent the inevitable tender spot. You may try one. However, I have found that I need actual contact with the needle on the underside to properly guide its direction. Never fear, a healthy callous will develop in no time.

Exactly how you quilt is not important, so long as you are constantly quilting toward an unquilted end. If you were to quilt both ends toward the middle, there would surely be a pucker in either the top or the backing. Generally, after a portion of the quilt is finished, it is rolled away from the quilter, decreasing the thickness of the quilt on the stretcher nearest her. When the end is reached, the frame can be turned (or the stretchers reversed). The quilt should be rerolled so that the center is again exposed. The quilting then continues toward the remaining unquilted end.

As you quilt, the left hand should periodically slide along the backing, checking for excess. Pins can be removed and reset, so long as the excess in the top or backing is constantly worked toward the unquilted ends. Remember that you have a 4″ excess waiting to be used if necessary.

As you "roll," it will be necessary to reset the pins attaching the quilt to the siderails. Practice will teach proper tension on the frame. A quilt too tightly stretched is as difficult to quilt as one which is too loose.

UNIT VIII
Chapter 6/Finishing the Quilt

Three Common Methods. There are at least three ways to finish the edges of a quilt. The most common are rolling the edge of the quilt top to the back, rolling the backing to the topside, or binding the edges with bias.

To roll the top border fabric to the backing, you must first trim the batting and backing to the desired finished edge. Trim the quilt top, allowing 1″ more for the seam allowance and the hem. Turn the quilt over so that the backing is showing. Turn under ½″ of the border fabric so that a narrow ½″ hem is formed. Pin and blindstitch, mitering corners, if possible.

If a decorative fabric has been used for the quilt backing, and you would like it to show, use the first method in reverse to obtain a ½″ border of the decorative fabric on the top.

In both of these methods, the rolled hem may be wider. Simply allow twice the desired width as you trim the seam allowance.

Binding is by far the most common method of finishing. Baste a line ½″ from the planned edge of the quilt. Carefully measure the seam allowance and trim away any excess beyond the ½″ from all three layers. Measure the perimeter of the quilt (distance around). Stitch and cut ample binding, 2″ wide, using the instructions for Jiffy Bias on page 104. On the topside of the quilt, lay the edge of the bias strip along the edge of the quilt and pin it in place. Make small pleats at the corners. If you are using 2″ bias, stitch the bias to the quilt in a ½″ seam, using the machine if you wish. Fold under ½″ on the loose edge of the bias. Turn it to the back of the quilt and blindstitch it in place. Notice that all of the layers of the quilt extend to the finished edge.

The Keepsake. You may wish to embroider, initial, and date the quilt in a corner, or you may choose to quilt your name in parallel quilting lines, ¼″ apart. If all else fails, at least sign the quilt with an indelible laundry marker. Some day your pride and joy may be a genuine antique and cherished by generations to come.

Old-time quilting was rich with tradition and superstition. Let's start a new one. Whether the quilt is a gift or for your own use, *the quilter gets the first nap under her elaborate creation.*

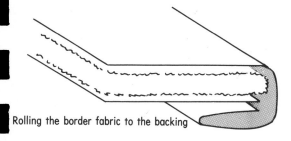

Rolling the border fabric to the backing

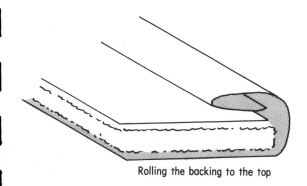

Rolling the backing to the top

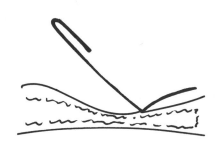

Finishing with bias binding

Appendix I   Jiffy Bias

Fabric Preparation

1 Cut a square of fabric (see estimates to determine how large a square will be needed).
2 Mark the lengthwise sides with 1 pin and the crosswise sides with 2 pins.

3 Fold the fabric in half diagonally and cut along the fold. You now have 2 triangles.

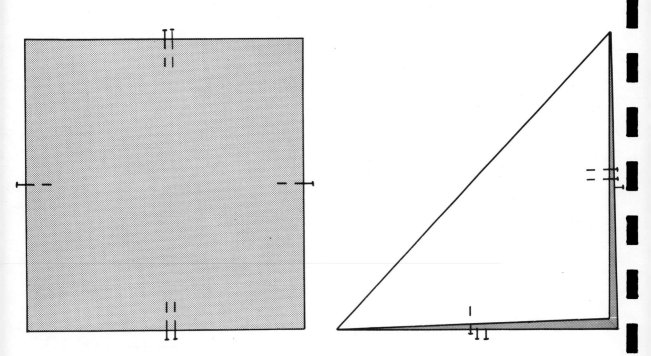

Sewing the Fabric

1 With the right sides together, sew the lengthwise sides (1 pin) together in a ¼″ seam. The pointed ends must be offset by ¼″ so that the edges will meet accurately at the actual seamline. Stitching must be done on the machine.

4 Bring point C over to point E. Laying the 2-pin edges together, pin point C to point E.
5 Pin all along the 2-pin edge. Point A will extend approximately 2¼″ past point B.
6 Stitch from B to C.

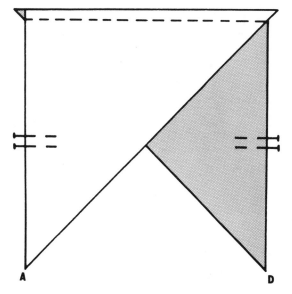

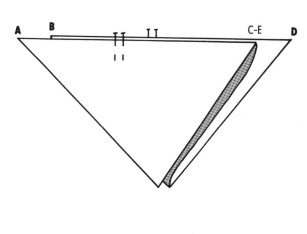

2 Pick up corner A and lift it up to open the fabric flat on the table.
3 Lay a ruler perpendicular to the bottom edge, C-D, and slide the ruler to the left from point D until the distance from C-D to B-D is 1½″. Mark this point E.

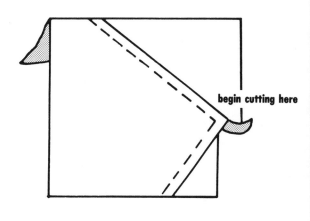

begin cutting here

Cutting. Begin cutting 1½″ wide bias at either extension. Use a ruler as a guide and continue cutting until all of the fabric is used.

105

Advanced technique: to facilitate even cutting, mark lines
parallel to the bias edge beginning at point E

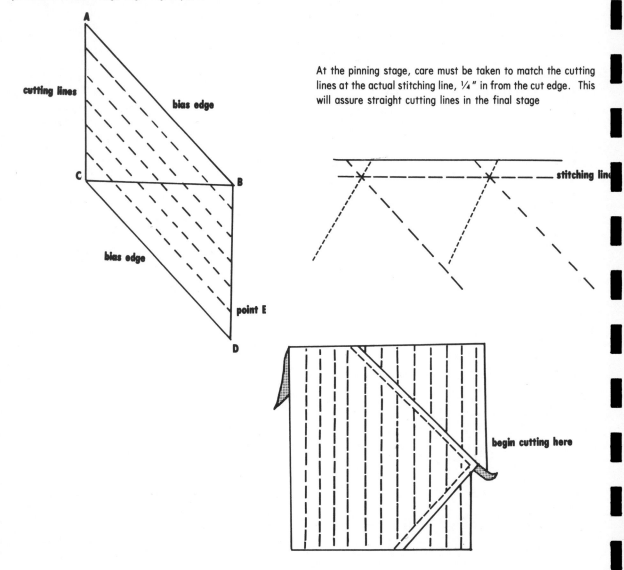

At the pinning stage, care must be taken to match the cutting
lines at the actual stitching line, ¼" in from the cut edge. This
will assure straight cutting lines in the final stage

Estimates for 1½" Wide Bias
Begin with a 12" square to obtain 2½ yards of bias
Begin with a 18" square to obtain 5½ yards of bias
Begin with a 36" square to obtain 18 yards of bias

Wider Bias. It is possible to make wider (or narrower)
bias simply by changing the distance from D to E
(sewing step #3) to the desired bias width.

Quilt Binding. A 44" square (minus selvages) will yield
approximately 25 yards of 2" wide bias binding.

Appendix II   Quilting Designs

Designs for Overall Quilting. Large empty areas, such as the center square in Simple Star, should be quilted. Unfortunately, such areas are rarely an even measurement which can be easily divided into subunits. If you decide to quilt diamonds or squares, for example, cut a strip of paper the actual length of one side of the square to be quilted. Fold it in half, quarters, eights, etc., until you reach the scale you desire. Unfold the strip and lay it along the seamline of the square. Using a washable marker, transfer marks to the fabric at each folding. Mark the other 3 sides of the square. Using a ruler, connect the markings to form the design you have selected.

For overlapping shells, mark lines for squares, using light dotted lines. Cut a half-circle from cardboard. Mark slash marks or cut small notches in the outer edge to indicate the points at which the designs should end or overlap. Mark the first row. Add additional rows, matching slash marks so that the shells are evenly spaced.

These simple designs may be used on borders, as well. These designs may be used on an appliqued block, but commonly the design does not continue over the applique itself.

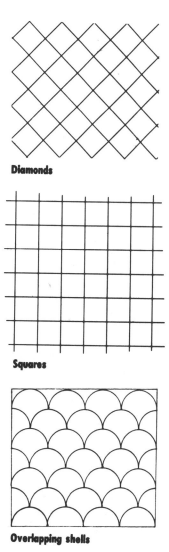

Diamonds

Squares

Overlapping shells

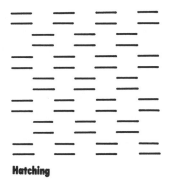

Hatching

Designs for Plain Blocks. If a quilt is set together with pieced or appliqued blocks alternating with plain blocks, the quilting on the plain blocks often duplicates the quilting on the other blocks.

Often an independent design is quilted on the plain blocks. Feathers, wreaths, and flower designs are both beautiful and traditional. You may quilt your initials in pairs of quilting lines ¼″ apart for a very personalized effect.

Designs for Borders and Lattice Strips. For borders and lattice strips, a template should be cut from cardboard, complete with notches for overlapping the design. How neatly the corners match or turn will be an important factor in the beauty of the back of the quilt.

If the lattice fabric is very dark and difficult to mark with quilting lines, try this simple approach. Quilt ½″ outside the blocks on the latticework, stitching a "frame" for each block. Then quilt down the center of the lattice. All of the quilting can probably be done with very little marking. Additional lines can be added as necessary.

Traditional Quilting. Remember that old quilts were heavily quilted. Rarely were spaces more than an inch. Although our modern-day batting allows us to skimp, for a more traditional feeling, never leave spaces of more than 2″. Of course, you must be the final judge as to just how much quilting is deemed ideal or necessary.

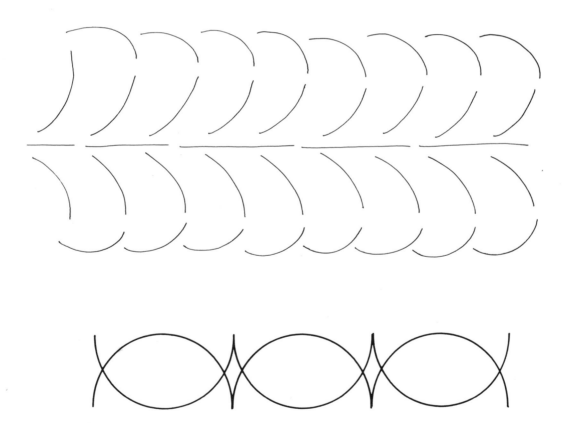

Permanent Template Section

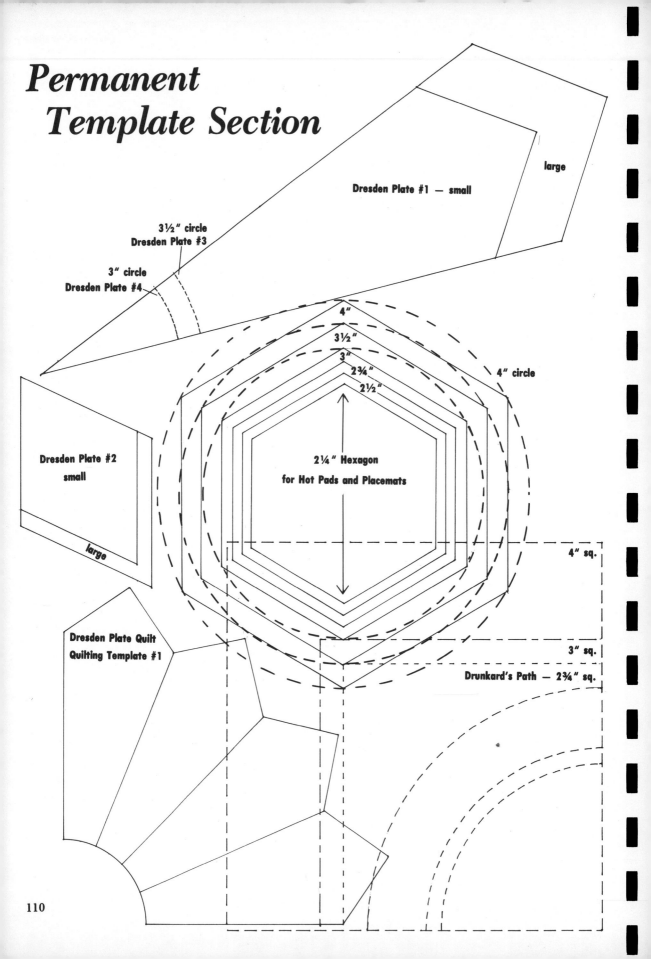

Dresden Plate #1 — small

large

3½" circle
Dresden Plate #3

3" circle
Dresden Plate #4

4"

3½"

3"

2¾"

2½"

4" circle

Dresden Plate #2
small

2¼" Hexagon
for Hot Pads and Placemats

large

4" sq.

Dresden Plate Quilt
Quilting Template #1

3" sq.

Drunkard's Path — 2¾" sq.

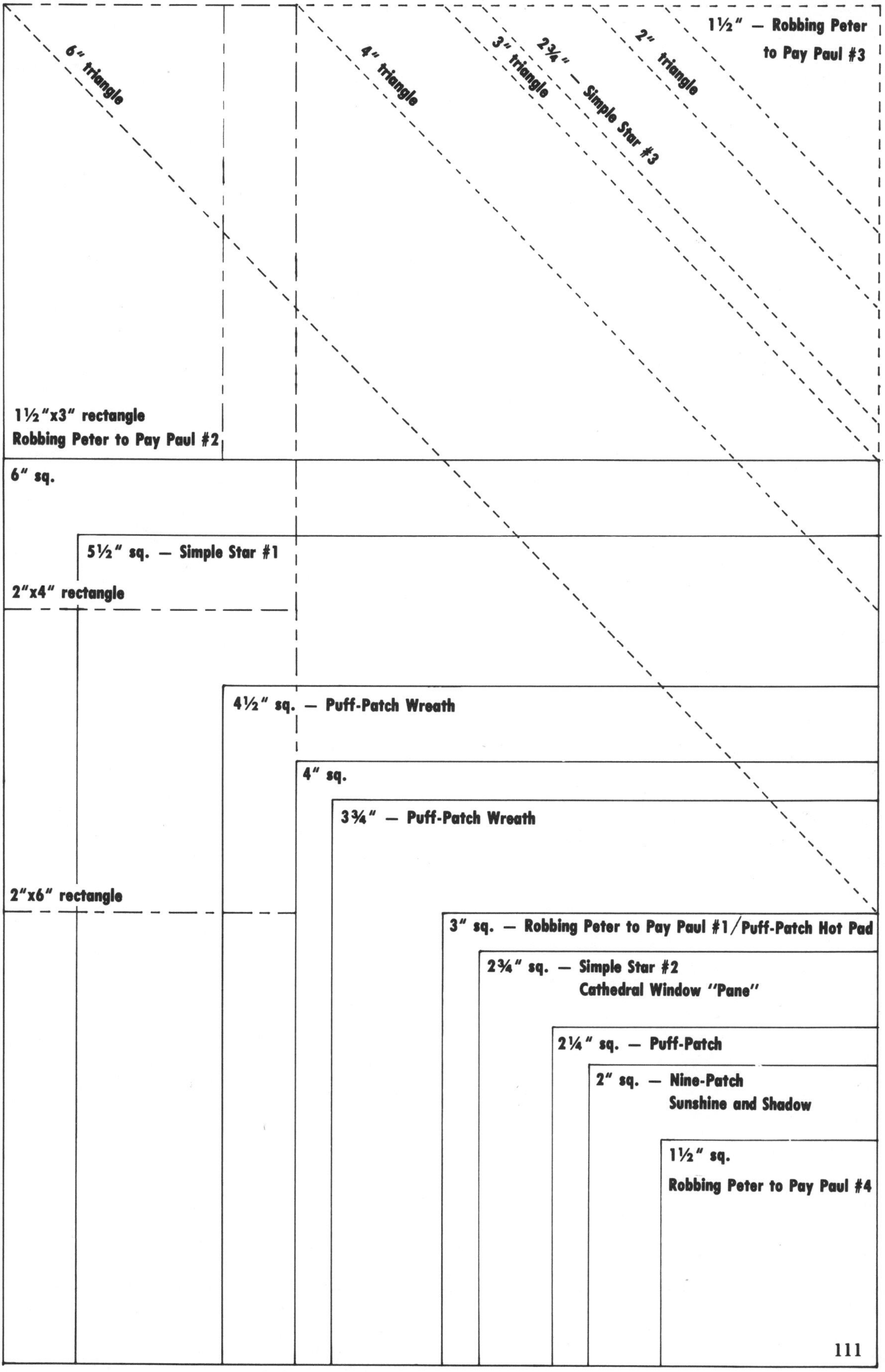

6" triangle

4" triangle

3" triangle

2¾" triangle — Simple Star #3

2" triangle

1½" — Robbing Peter
to Pay Paul #3

1½"x3" rectangle
Robbing Peter to Pay Paul #2

6" sq.

5½" sq. — Simple Star #1

2"x4" rectangle

4½" sq. — Puff-Patch Wreath

4" sq.

3¾" — Puff-Patch Wreath

2"x6" rectangle

3" sq. — Robbing Peter to Pay Paul #1/Puff-Patch Hot Pad

2¾" sq. — Simple Star #2
Cathedral Window "Pane"

2¼" sq. — Puff-Patch

2" sq. — Nine-Patch
Sunshine and Shadow

1½" sq.

Robbing Peter to Pay Paul #4

Unit V: Pella Tulip
Tracing Pattern for Applique Background

Diagonal Foldline

Horizontal or Vertical Foldline

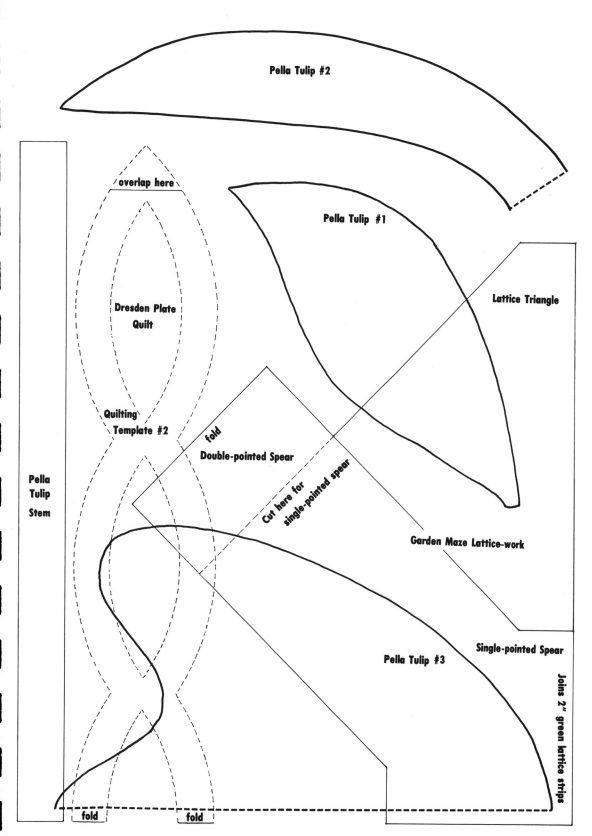

Pella Tulip #2

overlap here

Pella Tulip #1

Lattice Triangle

Dresden Plate
Quilt

Quilting
Template #2

fold

Double-pointed Spear

Cut here for
single-pointed spear

Pella
Tulip
Stem

Garden Maze Lattice-work

Single-pointed Spear

Pella Tulip #3

Joins 2" green lattice strips

fold   fold

Appendix IV   Helpful Hints

1 Preshrink all the fabrics to be used: for piecing, applique, quilt backing, pillow backing and decorative edging. Always use similar fabrics in piecework — the same weight and fiber content.

2 Keep 2 or 3 colors of thread in your quilting supply box for piecing. Beige, navy (not black), and red or orange should be acceptable for nearly all piecing. For applique, of course, matching thread is preferred.

3 Slide your piecing thread along a piece of beeswax to eliminate troublesome knotting.

4 Corners — stitch them well the first time. It's easier to do it right the first time than it is to patch things up each time the quilt comes out of the wash.

5 Quilt from the center out, center out, center out . . . .

6 Check your quilting stitch frequently. Keep striving for perfection. Check the following points:
   a. Number of stitches per inch.
   b. Stitch regularity and evenness.
   c. Do the stitches go through all of the layers?
   d. Tension.

7 Do not trim the project until the quilting is finished. Quilting sometimes distorts the top fabric, and minor adjustments are possible if there is sufficient allowance at the outer edges.

8 After you've made a sample block of your quilt, mark and cut out all the pieces you'll be needing. This will prevent running short of fabric when it is too late to buy more.

9 When you make templates for applique, be certain to extend the patterns so that the appliqued pieces overlap properly.

10 Never seam quilt backing down the middle of the quilt. If it is necessary to piece, add two strips, one to each side of the center panel.

11 Keep track of your *accomplishments* instead of your failures.

Glossary

Album Quilt: a sampler quilt made of blocks of a variety of patterns and/or sizes. Made by one person, or by several as a gift.

Applique: (noun) a cutout piece of fabric fastened to a larger piece of material.

(verb) to apply, as decoration, one piece to a larger piece of material.

Applique Background: the large piece of fabric to which the design is applied.

Backing: the bottom or lining layer of a quilt; it can be white, colored, or patterned. Muslin, with its low thread count is preferred.

Backstitch: the type of stitch taken at the beginning and end when one is stitching pieces together, and the reinforcing stitch used every third or fourth stitch to strengthen the running stitch. In short, after taking a stitch, reinsert the needle a stitch length to the right and bring it up a stitch length to the left.

Baste: to secure temporarily, either with a long running stitch (often in a contrasting thread color for visibility's sake) or with pins.

Batting: the filling for the quilt, often called "wadding"; it can be cotton or polyester. In addition to providing warmth, it enhances the quilting design because it swells on both sides of the quilting line, adding dimension.

Binding: a narrow fabric used to finish the raw edges of the quilt.

Blindstitch: a hemming stitch which does not show visible threads on the right side; ideal for applique. Take a stitch inside (and parallel to) the fold of the applique, take a second stitch in the applique background directly beneath the fold of the applique — as the thread is pulled taut, the stitch becomes invisible.

Blocks: a unit of piecework which is repeated to create an overall design on the quilt top. It can also refer to a single unit if it expresses a total idea.

Border: a single strip or piece of fabric or a complex unit of pieces used to enlarge a quilt top or to provide a decorative edge around the quilt design.

Calico: cotton fabric printed with figured patterns, originally from Calicut, India, from whence the name is derived.

Corded or Italian Quilting: consists of two layers with stitching in parallel lines, between which cords are inserted for a decorative effect. Often used in conjunction with Trapunto.

Coverlet: a blanket-sized bedcovering, not large enough to cover the pillows or extend to the floor. A coverlet is not necessarily quilted and may refer to any bed-covering.

Finger-rolling: a technique used to prepare appliques for blindstitching; the seam allowance is rolled under by the fingers of one hand as it is basted by the other.

Friendship Quilt: a quilt made up of blocks, each made by a different person; the blocks may be identical or individually created by each quilter.

Lattice Strips: strips of fabric which are added between quilt blocks to add size and to keep the pattern from running together; also called Sashing.

Miter: to join two strips (of fabric) by cutting the two strips at an angle and piecing them together; also, fabric can be folded on an angle to simulate a pieced miter.

Piece: (noun) a small section of fabric.

(verb) to sew small units of fabric together to make a larger unit.

Piecework: a unit made by sewing small pieces together to form a larger unit; the term used to differentiate this type from Applique.

Pillow Backing: the fabric which shows as the back of a finished pillow; it is not involved in the quilting process.

Pin-Baste: to secure temporarily using pins instead of thread.

Quilt: (noun) a bed coverlet of 2 layers of fabric filled with cotton, wool, or man-made fiber and held together by stitched designs.

(verb) to stitch or sew in layers with padding in between; to stitch, sew, or cover with lines or patterns like those used in quilts.

Quilt Top: the top layer of a quilt or quilted project; it can be pieced, appliqued, or of a single piece of fabric.

Quilting Frame: the frame used to hold a quilt's layers as it is being quilted; the large frame consists of 4 bars of wood: 2 stretchers and 2 side-rails. In "olden days," 2 stretchers were often used with 4 chairs; for small projects, an embroidery hoop or adjustable needlepoint frame is sometimes used. Quilting with no frame is possible on small projects if the quilter is mindful of tension.

Reverse Applique: a technique which is simply the reverse of traditional applique; designs are cut from the "applique background" to expose the fabric layer or layers underneath; carried to extremes, several layers can be combined and cut through so that a many-colored design is the result.

Sashing: see Lattice.

Scrapbag Quilting: the use of bits of scraps to create a quilt top, usually piecework rather than applique; each block may consist of a separate set of fabrics, or fabrics may be randomly scattered all over the top.

Square: (adj.) the quality of having exact right angles at the 4 corners.

(noun) a square piece of fabric; a quilt piece.

Stay-Stitch: machine-stitching along the seamline which reinforces the applique before clipping.

Template: the pattern from which pieces are cut.

Tied Coverlet: a coverlet with the wadded or layered construction of a quilt, but secured with ties at even intervals instead of stitching.

Trapunto: a form of quilting consisting of 2 layers of fabric with the stuffing used only in places to emphasize the design (the stuffing is inserted through tiny holes in the backing); also called Stuffed Quilting.

White-Work: a quilt top consisting of one bed-sized piece of cloth quilted in intricate designs; usually a bedspread rather than a blanket.

Index

A

Anvil, 86, 87
"Any Fool Can Do It" Pillow, 32-33
Applique, 47-51
  Background, 47
  Preparation for, 48, 70-73
  Reverse, 50
  Stitch, 49-50
Assembling Layers for Quilting, 22-23, 100
Attic Window, 82

B

Backing for the Quilt, 12
Backstitching, 20
Barbara Frietchie Star, 86, 88
Basting-in-Place, 73
Batting, 11-12
Bear Claws, 86, 87
Bear's Foot, 86, 87
Bear's Paw, 86, 87
Bear Tracks, 86, 87
Beeswax, 8
Bias, 10-11
Bias Binding, 37, 104-106
Bias Bows, 80-81
Binding, see Bias Binding
Biscuit Quilting, 76
Blindstitch, 49-50
Borders, 36-37
  Mitered, 37
  Simple, 36
  Quilt Designing, 94
Bows, 80-81
Bows and Arrows, 14
Burying the Knot, 24

C

Cathedral Window, 82-85
Centering Layers for Quilting, 100-101
Christmas Wreath, Puff-Patch, 77-81
Clamshell Quilting Design, 107
Clay's Choice, 86, 87, 98, 99
Colorfastness, 10
Cording, 37
Corn and Beans, 13
Country Husband, 14

Coverlet, Puff-Patch, 81
Cross and Crown, 86, 87
Curves, Marking and Piecing, 44-45
Cutting Method, 17

D

Determining Fabric Requirements, 95-97
Dolly Madison's Star, 89, 90
Dolly Madison's Workbox, 13, 14
Double Monkey Wrench, 13
Dresden Plate, 47
  Friendship Quilt, 69
  Pillow, 47-51
  Pillow Shams, 63
  Placemats, 51
  Quilt, 52, 52-64
  Template-making, 51
Drunkard's Path, 14, 22, 44, 86
  Pillow, 44-46
  Variations, 14, 45-46
Dual Template for Marking Right and Wrong sides of
  Fabric, 54
Duck and Ducklings, 13
Duck's Foot-in-the-Mud, 86, 87
Dutchman's Puzzle, 86, 87

E

Evening Starr, 86

F

Fabrics, 9-11
Fabric Markers, 8
Fabric Marking, 16
Fabric Preparation, 10
Falling Timber, 45
Finger-pressing, 27
Finger-rolling, 71-72
Finishing a Quilt, 103
Folded Miter, 28-29
Fool's Puzzle, 45
Frame-quilting, 100-102
Frames, 101-102
Friendship Quilt, 69
Fundamentals of Quilting, 26

G
Garden Maze Lattice, **74**, 74-75, 113
Goose Tracks, 86, **87**
Grainlines, 10-11
Grandmother's Fan, 69
Grandmother's Favorite, 89, 90
Grandmother's Flower Garden, 2, 39, **40, B. Cover**
    Hot Pad, Mosaic, 40-42
    Placemats, 42-43

H
Hand of Friendship, 86, **87**
Handy Andy, 13
Harry's Star, 86, **87**
Harvest Wreath, 81
Hemming Stitch, 49
Hen and Chickens, 13, 86, 88, 89
Henry of the West, 86, **87**
Hexagons, 39-43
    Diamonds, 39
    Grandmother's Flower Garden, 39
    Hot Pad, Mosaic, **40,** 40-42
    Ovals, 39
    Placemats, 42-43
    Stars, 39
    Using Striped Fabrics, 40
Hole-in-the-Barn-Door, 13
Hot Pads
    Nine-Patch, 27, 27-29
    Mosaic-Hexagon, 40-42
    Puff-Patch, 76-77
How to Use This Manual, 6

I–K
Ironing, 22
Jackson's Star, 86, **87**
Jiffy Bias, 104-106
Kentucky Rose, 89
Kitty-Corner, 13

L
Lap-Quilting, 52-64
Lattice, 89
Layers, Assembling for Quilting, 22-23, 100-102
    Basting, 23
    Pin-Basting, 23
Lincoln's Platform, 13
Log Cabin, 19, **22**
Love Knot, 13
Love Ring, 14

M
Marking the Fabric, 16
Marking Utensils, 8
Mattress Dimensions, 91-92

Mayflower, 86, 88
Mexican Star, 89
Mill Wheel, 45
Mini-Pillow, 29
Miter, Folded, 28-29
Monkey Wrench, 13
Mosaic Hot Pad, 40-42
Multi-Template, 42

N
Needles, 7
Nine-Patch, 27, 27-33
Nomenclature, 13-14
Nonesuch, 14

O
Oak Leaf, 89
Octagon, 14
One-Pin Method of Pinning, 36
Oval **Flower Garden** Placemats, **42-43**

P
Paper-Pressing, Applique, 71
Pella Tulip, F. Cover, 2, **70**
    Pillow, 70-74
    Quilt, 74-75
Permanent Template Section, 110-113
Piecing
    Curves, 44-46
    Dresden Plate, 48
    General Instructions, 17-21
    Hexagons, 40-41
    Order, 19
    Squares, 27
    Stitch, 20
    Triangles, 35-38
Pierced Star, 86, **88**
Pillow Filling, 12
Pillow-Making, 30-33
    Circular, 50
Pillows
    Cathedral Window, 82-85
    Dresden Plate, 47-51
    Drunkard's Path, 44-46
    Nine-Patch, 27-28
    Pella Tulip, 70-74
    Puff-Patch, 81
    Robbing Peter to Pay Paul, 38
    Simple Star, 35-37
    Sunshine and Shadow, 33-34
Pillow Shams, **Dresden Plate,** 63
Pin-Basting, 23
Pins, 7
Piping, Ready-made, 30
Placemats
    Oval **Flower Garden,** 42-43
    Dresden Plate, 51

Polyester Filling, 12
Pot Holders, see Hot Pads
Powdered Blueing, 8
Preshrinking, 10
Puff-Patch, 76-81
   Christmas Wreath, 77
   Coverlet, 81
   Harvest Wreath, 81
   Hot Pad, 76
   Machine-Piecing, 78-79
   Pillow, 81
Puss-in-the-Corner, 13

Q
Quartering and Centering Quilting Layers,
   100–101
Quilt Backing, 12
Quilt Batting, 11
Quilting Designs, 107-109
   Borders and Lattice Strips, 109
   Clay's Choice, 99
   Dutch designs, 75
   Feathers, 108-109
   Hexagons, 43
   Marking, 8, 98
   Overall Quilting, 107
   Plain Blocks, 108
   Wreath, 108
Quilting Needles, 7
Quilting Thread, 8
Quilting Stitch, 24-26
   Burying the Knot, 24
   Ending Quilting Thread, 25
Quilt-making
   Design, 86-90
   Fabric Determination, 95-97
   Finishing, 103
   Frame-quilting, 100-102
   Mathematics, 91-94
   Quilt Top, 98-99
   Sizes, 91-93
Quilts
   Grandmother's Flower Garden, 2, **B. Cover**
   Dresden Plate, 52, 52-64
   Friendship, 69
   Pella Tulip, 74

R
Reverse Applique, 50
Robbing Peter to Pay Paul, 13-14, 86
   Pillow, 38
Rocky Road to California, 14
Rocky Road to Dublin, 14
Ruffles, 31
   Double, 32, 34
Running Stitch, 20

S
Sailboat, 86, **88**
Scissors, 7
Sewing Box, 7
Sherman's March, 13
Shoo-Fly, 13
Shopping List, 121
Shrinkage Factor, 91
Simple Star, 35, 35-37, 86
Squares, Piecing
   General Instructions, 15-21
   Nine-Patch, 27, 27-28
   Sunshine and Shadow, 33, 33-34
Stacking and Threading, 17, 34
Star of the West, 86, **87**
Stay-stitching, 73
Steeplechase, 14
Straightening Fabric, 10
Striped Fabric, Hexagons, 40
Stuffing for Pillows, 12
Sunshine and Shadow, 33, 33-34
Supplies, 7-12

T
Template Cardboard, 12
Template Cutting, 15-16
Templates
   Cut-out Section, 123-135
   Dual, 54
   Multi-template, 42
   Permanent Section, 110-113
   Window, 40
Tension, Quilting Stitch, 25
The Great Iowa Quilt Factory, 2, 69
Thimbles, 9
Thread, 9
Tic-Tac-Toe, 13
Tooth-Fairy Pillow, 29
Triangles
   Marking and Cutting, 35
   Piecing, 36
   Problem-Solving, 38
   Robbing Peter to Pay Paul, 38
   Simple Star, 35, 35-36
Trip Around the World, 33
Two-Pin Method, Piecing, 17-18

W
Winding Ways, 14
Wind Mill, 86, **87**
Window Templates, 40
Wreath
   Christmas, **Puff-Patch,** 77-81
   Harvest, **Puff-Patch,** 81
   Quilting Design, 108
Wreath of Pansies, 89

About the Author

It will be immediately apparent to the reader of *You Can Be a Super Quilter!* that Carla J. Hassel is a gifted, inspiring teacher of exceptional ability who has full mastery of her subject and the rare talent to write clearly and instructively about it.

Born in Elmhurst, Illinois, Carla grew up in Dubuque, Iowa, and now makes her home in Des Moines with attorney-husband Gary and children Kirsten and David.

Her college years were spent at Knox College, Galesburg, Illinois, where she was granted a B.A. degree following a four-year pre-med curriculum. She attributes to this training her "scientific approach to quilting and everything else, I guess."

In addition to teaching quilting, she has also taught classes in International Cooking to children and adults and is currently teaching German to second graders through a school volunteer program. When time permits, travel, music (she plays cello and piano), and *wallpapering* are activities she most enjoys.

About the philosophy that underlies her writing, Carla stated, "What I try to project is a problem-solving approach to quilting. Figure out what needs to be done and then figure out *how* to do it. After finishing this book the reader-quilter should be ready to tackle pattern drafting, extensive color technique, and the most challenging pieced and appliqued designs."

In other words, she'll truly be a Super Quilter!

TEAR-OUT TEMPLATE SECTION

Tear Here

Shopping List

Sewing Box
Needles: Sharps—7 or 8
            Betweens—7 and 8 (9 and 10, if available)
Pins: Ballpoint size 17 or Dressmaker size 17 or 20,
       plastic head preferred
Scissors: A small pair for thread-cutting to be kept in
           the box
           Template-cutting scissors
           Dressmaking shears
Thread
Beeswax
Fabric Markers: Light-colored pencil—#2½ or #3
                 Washable, felt-tip pen
Rulers: 6″ for the sewing box; 18″ for home use
Tape Measure
Pincushion
Thimble
Seam Ripper
Manila Envelope: 6½″ x 9½″
Colored Pencils
Graph Paper
Loose-leaf Binder
Lined Notebook
Fabric for Tops
Polyester or Cotton Quilt-batting: twin or full size
Quilt Backing: 1 yard, 80″ to 90″ wide muslin sheeting
Polyester Filling
Template Cardboard: Index cards for small templates
                    Large sheet of poster board (32″
                    x 40″) for quilt-sized templates

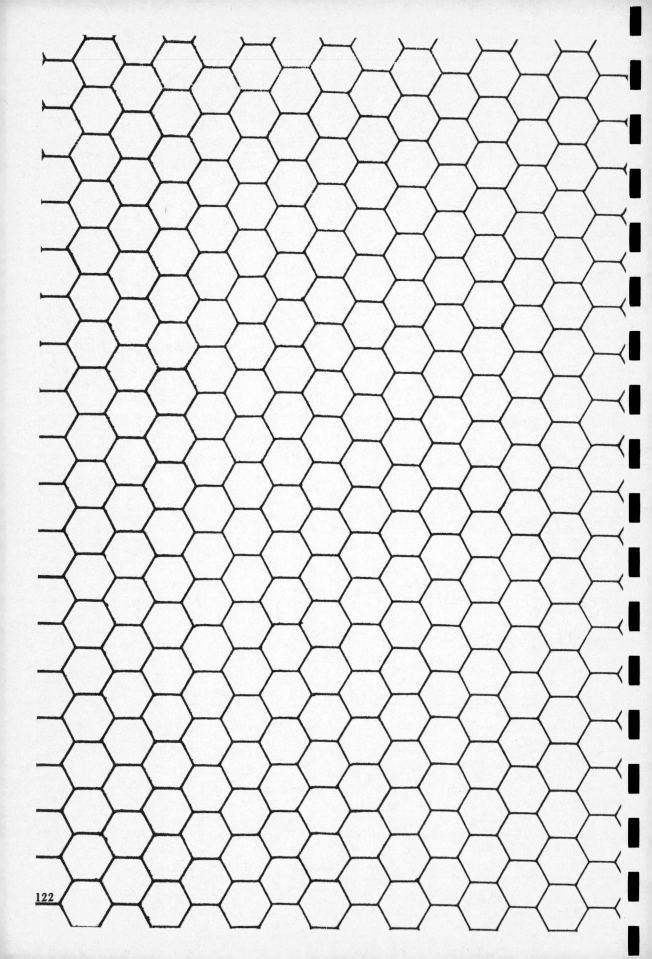

Tear Here

#2 Simple Star

2″ sq.

Nine-Patch

Sunshine and Shadow

#1 Simple Star

124   Patrick's Quilt 1979

#2
Robbing Peter to Pay Paul

#1   Robbing Peter to Pay Paul

#3   Simple Star

#4
Robbing Peter to Pay Paul

#3
Robbing Peter
to Pay Paul

#1   Drunkard's Path

#2   Drunkard's Path

Hexagon

126

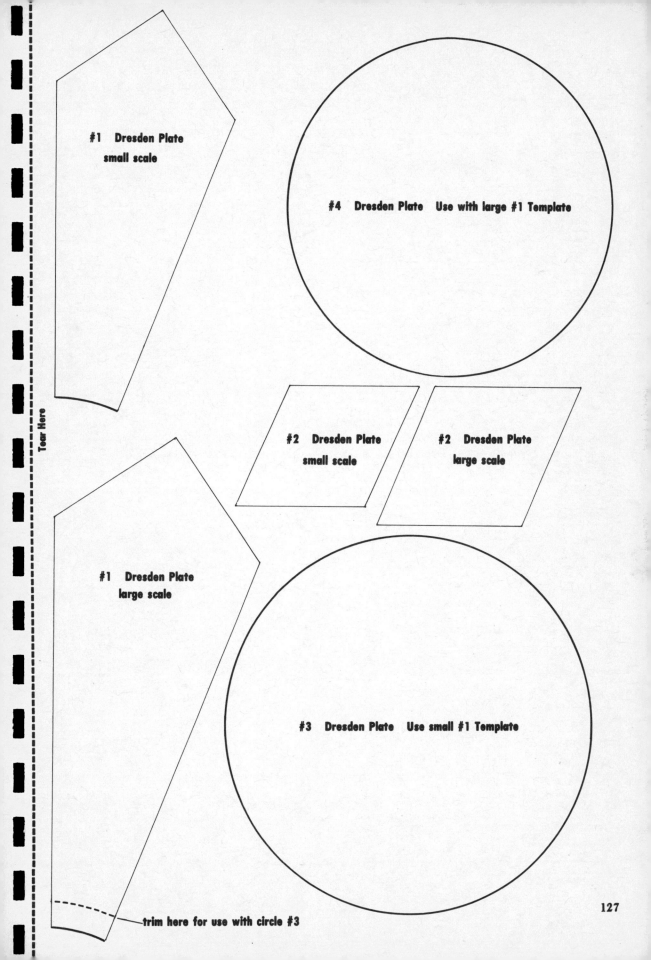

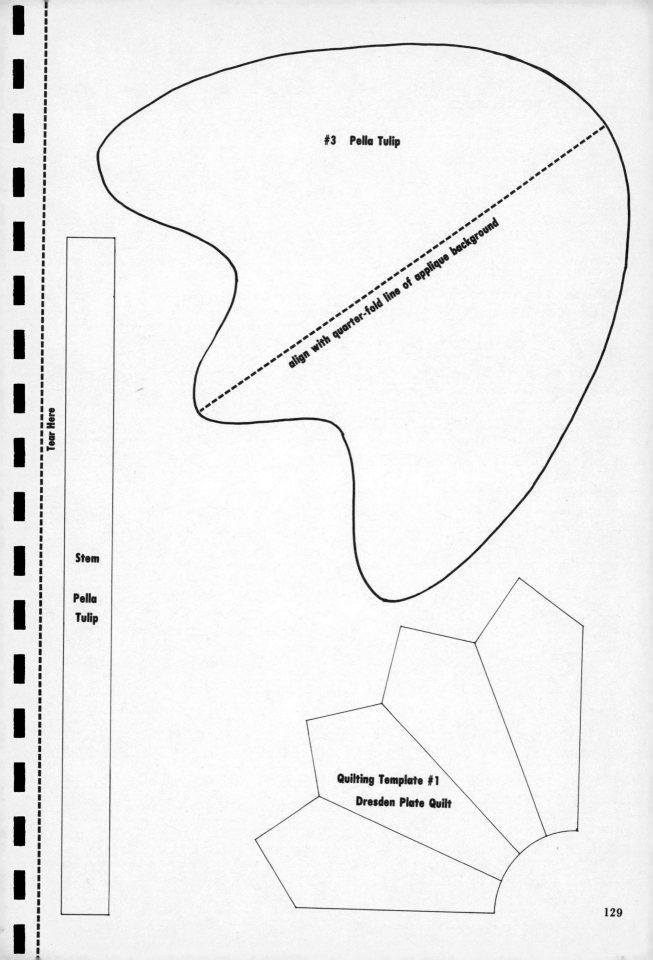

#3   Pella Tulip

align with quarter-fold line of applique background

Stem

Pella

Tulip

Quilting Template #1

Dresden Plate Quilt

130

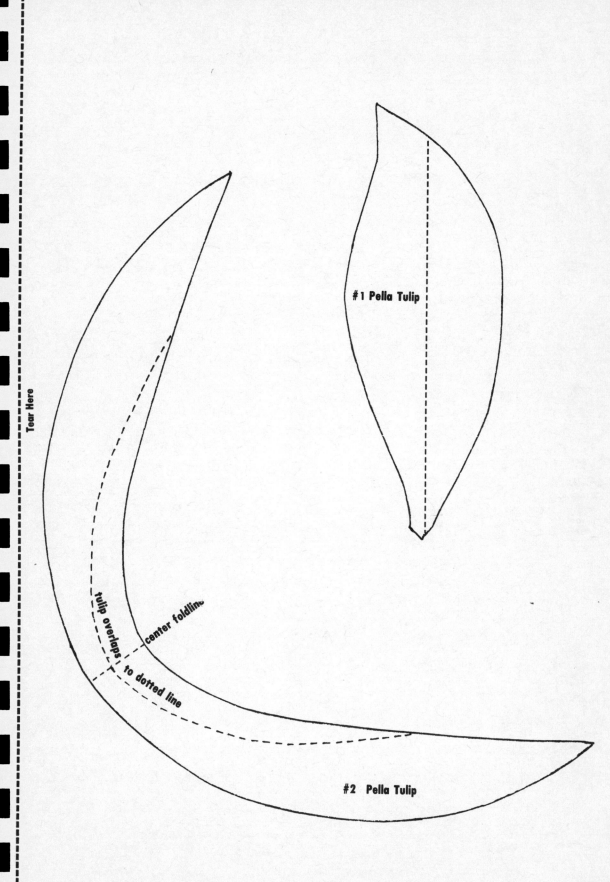

#1 Pella Tulip

tulip overlaps

center foldline

to dotted line

#2 Pella Tulip

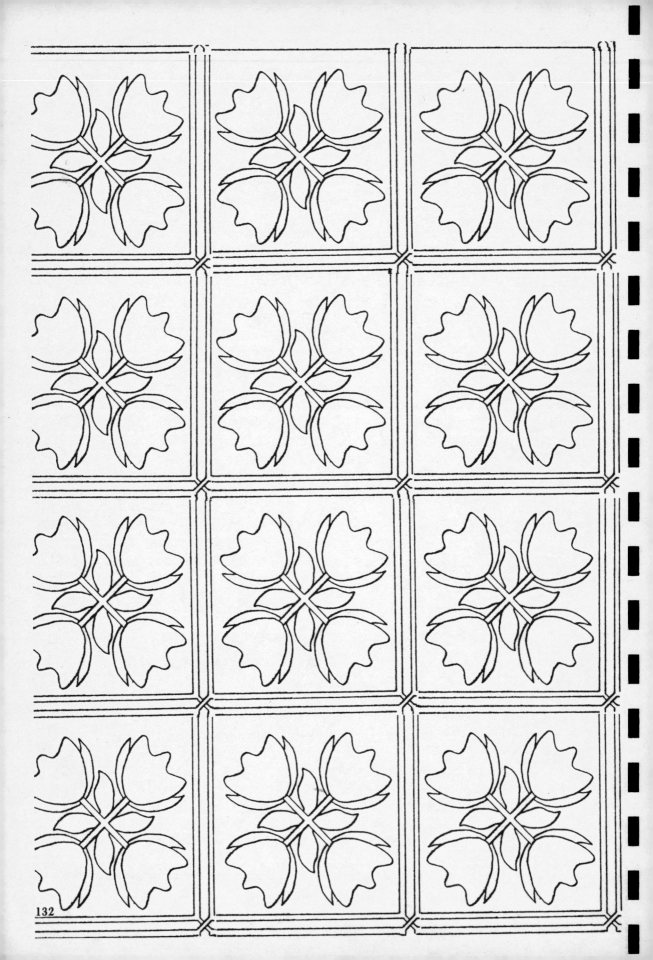

132

overlap here
to extend

Quilting Template #2
Dresden Plate Quilt

Cut on fold

Top
Puff-Patch Hot Pad
3" sq.

Backing
Puff-Patch Hot Pad
2¼" sq.

Pane
Cathedral Window
2¾" sq.

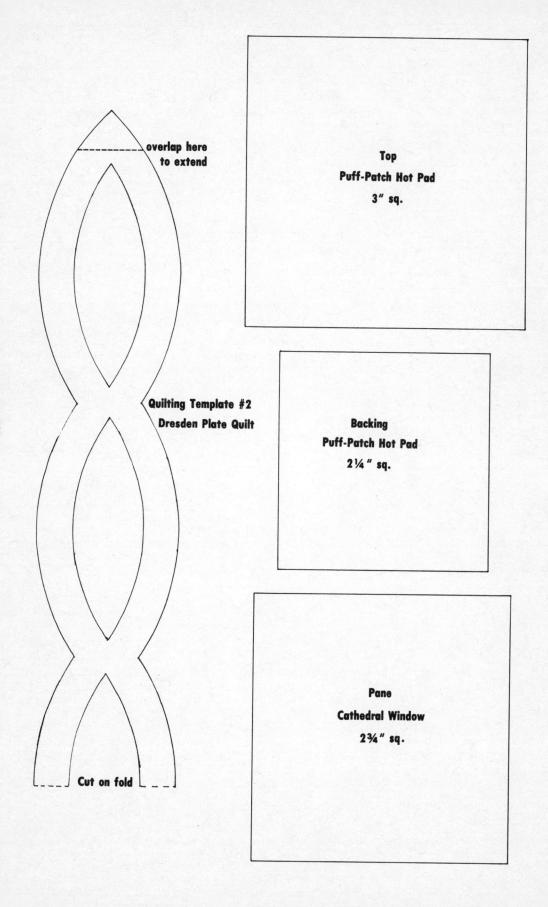

Backing
Puff-Patch Wreath
3¾" sq.

Top
Puff-Patch Wreath
4½" sq.